Granny

P.I.

By Nancy A. Wilson

First paperback edition September 2020.

ISBN 978-1-7356702-0-1 (paperback)
ISBN 978-1-7356702-1-8 (ebook)

| | HERBIVORE PRESS

For inquiries: Howdy@HerbivorePress.com

Foreword

Nancy Wilson was a pistol. I say she was because, sadly, she unexpectedly passed away in May of 2019. She left behind an unfinished draft of *Granny P.I.*, a manuscript she had  written to memorialize some of the crazy characters, wild adventures, and good old-fashioned sleuthing that occurred throughout a career that spanned more than forty years as a self-proclaimed "Lady Private Investigator."

Eighty years old at the time of her passing, she was still actively working cases, albeit much less frequently, through her company Wilson & Wilson Investigations. She started the firm in 1984 with her husband, Don Wilson, having learned the trade working as an insurance investigator almost ten years before. When Don died in 1995, Nancy continued to run the firm, maintaining Wilson & Wilson's stellar reputation for busting insurance fraud and finding individuals who didn't want to be found.

The firm kept a steady clientele comprised primarily of insurance companies, but, especially in the early years, they took on all sorts of cases, including more perilous assignments. One can only imagine the stories we'd learn if Nancy would have finished the section she titled "Threats," with curious chapters and case descriptions such as "Murder in Jennings," "Rape in Peal River," and "$200,000. In Cash. In His Briefcase."

The only specific threat she did detail there she included in the case called "Guy Cleaning Gun in Houma," where she describes her assignment to get a statement from said guy's wife while he stared directly at her, asking if she liked guns and wanting to know if she happened to shoot them, use one, or carry one. While some investigators insist that their work is nothing like the danger portrayed in the movies, these types of threats and the high-crime areas her cases required her to frequent were the reasons Nancy kept her concealed handgun permit up to date.

To fully appreciate the book's title, what you need to know about Nancy is that she was sharp as a tack, rather obstinate, a bit prone to braggadocios, and had a very distinct speaking cadence and a body that had been significantly impacted over the last ten to fifteen years of her life with a bad case of scoliosis. The condition left her with a fairly significant bend in her back that caused her to walk with a cane. Not happy that the scoliosis had left her barely five feet tall, throughout her seventies, she insisted on wearing shoes with two-inch wedge heels to give her extra height, much to the chagrin of her daughters.

Not only did Nancy not let her condition stop her from working, but she also used it to her advantage as she continued conducting surveillance and serving subpoenas. She loved to tell stories of how unexpected fraudsters willingly opened the door for the supposed "little old lady" with her cane and her dog, who then didn't know what hit them when she proudly announced that they had been served!

Based in Baton Rouge, her work took her all over Southern Louisiana, deep in the heart of Cajun country, an area full of colorful characters with a unique culture unlike anywhere else in the country. Her assignments often took her to especially gritty neighborhoods, given her specialty for tracking down unsavory characters suspected of fraud and other criminal activities. Nancy often bragged about the role that Sally, the smartest dog ever, at least as far as she was concerned, played in her cases. "Shotgun Sally," as she was dubbed due to her ubiquitous spot riding shotgun in Nancy's red sports car, had a bark like a German shepherd, which you would never expect from her small size. She served as Nancy's sidekick, prop when needed, and loyal protector, ensuring no matter how unsavory the area where she was parked, no one would dare approach the car.

There is very little research regarding the exact number of female private investigators, with some studies suggesting that only about fifteen percent of all private investigators in the U.S. are women. The industry is extremely male-dominated, and this was certainly the case forty-plus years ago when Nancy began her career, making her an accomplished investigator and female business owner well before her time.

The early tales that she recounts go as far back as the '70s. Many of the stories don't include specific dates, but the time is evident in clues such as a bell-bottom ensemble described in a case where Nancy posed as a band promoter. In that story, she candidly recounts that back then, as a white female, there's no way she could have shown up alone in the evening at a black nightclub without raising ire or suspicion and thus she had to think of a more crafty approach to get into that club during daytime hours to get the information she needed.

These were different times, in a part of the country that even today continues to be rife with racial injustice, socioeconomic disparities, and gender inequality. People regularly assumed that Don, her husband whom she trained in the business, was her boss even though she ran the firm. Her stories illustrate how she was often underestimated and discounted, first as a young female in the field and over the years as a "Granny P.I." But just as she leveraged her age and fragile form in the latter part of her career, she used the gender stereotypes and assumptions that people made about her to her advantage to get the job done. She'd make a plan, develop the ruse, and then she'd play the part that would engender trust and gain rapport to disarm a witness, to get the ex-wife to spill the beans, or to convince an interviewee to tell more than they'd intended.

Unfortunately, as she did not have a chance to complete the book, many of her stories will remain untold. We are left to wonder precisely what Nancy encountered during an assignment to serve a subpoena in the case she named "Serving Breasts." We won't get to know what antic she was going to share in the case she called, "Gov. Edwards' Daughter." But her forty years as an investigator did result in some crazy stories that shed light on her sense of humor, her skills as an investigator, and the nature of the profession itself.

We hired a copy editor to fix some inevitable grammar issues and typos and re-ordered the sequence in which the stories are presented, but other than that, we left Nancy's work exactly as she left it. As such, it's probably worth noting that some of these stories may not be what some would term "politically correct," but these are her words, her experiences, and her actual memories in the spirit of the time, for better or worse. Under no circumstances would she have wanted us to edit accordingly—and if you know Nancy, you know exactly what we mean by this.

If you are a friend or family member of Nancy's, we hope reading this makes you laugh, makes you remember her for the unique character she was, and gives you some insight that you might not have had about the work she did so well that made her so proud over so many years. If you are a reader who didn't know Nancy, we hope that reading this entertains you as you get to hear her voice and see Granny P.I. in action, which will undoubtedly shed some light on why we called her a pistol and on what it's like to be a "Lady Private Investigator."

As Nancy would say, "It is a Most. Excellent. Profession!"

LOUISIANA STATE BOARD OF PRIVATE INVESTIGATOR EXAMINERS

This is to certify

Nancy J Wilson

is a licensed PRIVATE INVESTIGATOR representing

Wilson & Wilson Investigations

Baton Rouge   LA   Exp: 11/30/2002

LIC# 0954-113093-LA

EXECUTIVE DIRECTOR

DL# 001206607 LA

WILSON & WILSON
INVESTIGATIONS

NANCY A. WILSON
Owner/Investigator

30 Years Experience

CONCEALED HANDGUN PERMIT
GP17017076

LOUISIANA
DEPARTMENT OF PUBLIC SAFETY
AND CORRECTIONS

ISSUED: 11-18-2002
EXPIRES: 11-18-2004

DEPUTY SECRETARY

DL/ID: 001206607
DL/ID ST: LA **HAIR:** GRY **EYES:** HZL
SEX: F **HT:** 5-02 **WT:** 115
DOB: 11-24-1938

NANCY A WILSON
BATON ROUGE LA
70817-0000

12

Table of Contents

SURVEILLANCE..**15**

Crippled by Day. Swinging by Night......................16

Grocery Guy..21

Blind Fishing Guide..25

Bull in a China Shop......................................35

Deer, Squirrel, and Bear..................................38

Deer Club President..43

Kidnapping for The Colonel................................48

BBQ Shrimp on The Gulf....................................55

Lost Cat..59

Speaking of Cats..63

The Broken Ankle Hopper...................................66

Wal-Mart Pusher...69

STATEMENTS..**73**

Drunk & Disabled..74

House for Sale in Mandeville..............................78

All's Fair in Love and Nakedness.........................85

Wives & Girlfriends.......................................90

Where the Buffalo Roam....................................93

Bad Apple in this Bunch...................................99

Mississippi Mutt...105

Ragin' Cajun..108

Contacts...110

Lesbians and Pervert Attorneys.............................115

He Wore His Best Orange Coveralls.....................120

Murder One...122

Four Men and a Car...126

Body Odor, Smoke Smells & Lice........................129

New Orleans Ladies...133

SUBPOENAS...137

Serving the Mafia...138

Was it a Him? She? Or Shim?...............................142

Kicked Out of Dodge..147

Subpoena Vaccine..150

What are Sons-in-Law For?....................................153

My Other Body Guard?...155

Serving the Lowlives...157

SHOTGUN SALLY..159

The Ard-Angel..160

The Pickers, the Stinkers, and the Violent...........164

Horse...168

Would you Like to Meet my Dog?.........................171

PostScript..177

SURVEILLANCE

Wilson & Wilson, in the early days.

Nancy and Don Wilson "on assignment."

Crippled by Day. Swinging by Night.

This was one of the first cases that was assigned to me in my early years in the business, while I was working as an insurance investigator before we started our firm. Rayne is a small town in Cajun country, and our claimant, Bryson Brooks, was on a continuing disability income program. We had a tiny local office with one investigator, Larry Thibodeaux. A common practice at that time was for the investigator to provide a yearly update as to the activities of claimants to determine if they were working or not. Each year Larry would get this assignment, and each year he would report that Mr. Brooks was observed walking in this small town with crutches during the day, certainly not working.

My new supervisor, Earl Webster, decided to try out the new-kid-on-the-block and sent me over to Rayne to check old Mr. Brooks out. I drove the eighty-plus miles there, making inquiries and checking with my various sources of information I was beginning to develop, and got several leads that Mr. Brooks was the keyboard player in a band playing music at local clubs several nights a week. As I said, this was many years ago, in the early 1970s. Mr. Brooks was a black male, and I am a white female. In those days, I could never have gotten away with going to a black club—especially in a small town in south Louisiana.

My Assignment: Think of another way to confirm that Mr. Brooks did, in fact, play music, at night, in local clubs.

The Plan: In those years, my stepson also played music in a quite popular '50s music band. On the way back to Baton Rouge, I devised what I thought would be a pretty foolproof plan.

My Next Assignment: Convince my new supervisor to go along with that plan. Unfortunately, Earl was not too keen on the idea, but I convinced him to let me give it a shot. He ended the conversation with a big-time warning that if it even looked like I was going to have a problem, abort! And, for God's sake, be careful.

I needed several days to work this case to have any chance for success, so we needed the okay for the costs from our client. Once we got that approval, I gathered up several pamphlets for Back in the '50s Again, my stepson's band, grabbed some convincing folders, a binder, and some other tools I could use in the role of band promoter, and back to Rayne I went.

First, I had to do some background on Mr. Brooks, such as getting the name of his group and finding out where they performed. I had obtained a photo ID from the Department of Motor Vehicles and, after checking public records at the parish seat under Mr. Brooks' name (side note, we are parishes in Louisiana, not counties), I found that he had a mortgage of some band equipment with Terms Credit, a local lender. One of the first things we learn in this business is that you have to make a friend of your contact for the most part before you can get useful information. That is very easy to do in Cajun country because those are some of the nicest folks you would ever want to meet, and they want so much to be helpful, especially to outsiders. In speaking with the good manager at Terms Credit, he confirmed that Mr. Brooks was, indeed, a customer—sometimes behind in his monthly notes, but still a customer. And he told me exactly what else I needed to know.

"Yeah, he play music! De play at Bobby's Blues Club all da time! De pretty damn good, too!"

I next found out that Bobby's Blues Club doesn't open until 9 p.m. In checking with neighboring businesses, I found out that the club manager is Jimmy Boucher and that he's generally there around 3 p.m. I changed into my "band promoter" clothes, consisting of well-pressed bell-bottom jeans with a red turtleneck,

jean jacket, and hat, plus red boots. Shortly after 3 p.m.
I walked into Bobby's Blues Club, somewhat nervous. I
went up to the bartender, and he asked if he could help
me. I told him I would like to see Mr. Boucher if he was
in. He was.

He was in his office up the stairs. I made my way up
and knocked on the office door and was invited in. I
introduced myself and advised that I was representing
the band Back to the '50s Again and had heard that the
group called Black and Blues was quite popular in the
area. We were planning a concert in a couple of months
locally and were interested in getting a few local groups
to perform. Mr. Boucher wanted to know what he could
do for me. I told him we had heard that Black and Blues
had a favorable following locally and wanted to get his
opinion of them. He said that they were popular locally
and he would recommend them.

During this conversation, I had displayed the Back
in the '50s Again logo and also pulled out paperwork
to make it look very official. I explained that I needed
to know what kind of money they make, how they were
paid, how many were in the band, and the names of the
band members. Mr. Boucher could not wait to supply
this information. I told him it would also be helpful if

he could share what nights they played, how long they had been playing there, and what time they usually started. I asked if he could provide some background on each band member, such as how long each has been with the group. I asked him if I could have one of their posters, which he happily provided. Lastly, I asked for the names of other clubs where Black and Blues play so we could get additional recommendations to present to our people, and he gave us the name of three other local clubs.

With the information in hand that proved our claimant's activity level, I went back to Baton Rouge and had a "put up" (that's what we used to call going over an assignment) with Earl, who just shook his head.

"Sometimes, when you are a rookie, you are too stupid to know when and when not to proceed," he told me. "Sometimes it works, but usually it doesn't. Nancy, you were lucky this time."

No, Earl, I was smart!

The only negative was that poor old Larry Thibodeaux, the local investigator who originally had this case, hated my guts from then on. Can't blame him. For ten years, he'd been sending in his yearly reports confirming Mr. Brooks was on crutches and not working

Grocery Guy

I'm frequently asked if I've ever been threatened or scared. Not very often. More so in my early days than now, as I've learned from experience.

Years ago, way before Wilson & Wilson, I was trying to locate a fellow in Livingston Parish. In the process of doing so, I quickly learned that he, as well as much of his kin, had no problem with unethical, at best, and strongly criminal, at worst, behavior. Grandpa was that way. Dad was that way. The children were that way. It was a way of life.

As I said, this was very early in my career when I was very much the novice. I had not yet been able to find my subject, but I had a legal description of his property, which was something like "lot l, square 19, Hudson Subdivision." In those days, I didn't know how to convert that into a municipal address, but I didn't have any trouble locating the subdivision. I did learn that my man, Ray Bellingham, had a brother, Johnny Bellingham.

Johnny and their dad ran Bellingham Grocery right on the main highway. In passing the grocery store, I noticed there was an old car with a For Sale sign on it parked by the store. A big sign read, "Buy Your Groceries and Cars Here." Not thinking things through, I went into the grocery store and said I was looking for a used car for my son. I figured I could get into a casual conversation and ultimately get the information I needed. You know, like Rockford and Magnum do on TV. In hindsight, I made a bunch of really bad moves that day, but I hadn't learned enough yet to know that these were all stupid things to do.

1. I was a strange female in a small town, popping into a mom-and-pop grocery store inquiring about an old used car parked there. I'm blushing with embarrassment as I write this! I walked into the store and asked the first person I saw working in there about the car. Turned out to be brother Johnny. He said he could help me, and we walked out to the old vehicle.

2. I asked Johnny to start her up. He did. Smoke poured out of the exhaust, and it sounded as though it was going to fall apart. I told him that I was sure my son would be interested. Why in the world would this strange woman even consider this broken-down piece of car and not even ask how much he wanted for the thing?

3. I next announced that I was in real estate sales and was looking for a property owned by Ray Bellingham, and did he have any idea where that property might be? I did not even slide into the next subject, just changed topics in the middle of the stream. I could immediately tell he was just a tad more than slightly suspicious. He started telling me where it was, and I knew he was giving me a big runaround.

4. Then I made another big-time blunder, thinking that I would make myself look less suspicious. I asked if he knew Lloyd Clausen, who was an actual realtor I knew from the area. Sure enough, old Johnny knew Lloyd well. Do not, repeat, do not bring up other people's real names in such conversations, especially in small towns!

5. I thanked him, said I'd give the car info to my son and send him around. Then I left and drove back down the highway, not even making a pretense of going in the direction brother told me to go. Seriously, at least make it look like you're following up on what the guy told you.

By that time, I knew I had screwed up royally. But I didn't realize just how royally until later that afternoon when I got a call from, you guessed it, Lloyd Clausen. He had apparently pulled up to get gas at Bellingham Grocery right after I'd left. It seems Johnny asked Lloyd if he knew Nancy Wilson. "Sure," Lloyd said, "I know her."

Johnny asked, "What kind of work does she do?"

Lloyd responded, "Oh, she's some kind of investigator."

Johnny said, "Well, she's looking for my brother, and you tell her if she ever shows up back here, I'll kill her!"

I still go extremely fast when I go down the highway past Bellingham Grocery.

Blind Fishing Guide

We received this assignment in the early days of Wilson & Wilson Investigations. This was a brand-new client, an attorney with a large law firm in New Orleans. Walter Broussard called us saying that our best customer, a large insurance company, had recommended us in this case, and he wanted to meet with us personally. After meeting Walt, we had a good feeling about each other from the beginning. The claimant, Peter Bardin, was working offshore when he fell and hit his head on some pipe on ship. Walter explained that there were big bucks involved. Bardin had been offered a half-million dollars, which, in those days, was a whole lot of money. He was holding out for one million, claiming he had been blinded as a result of the injury.

Our Assignment: Mr. Bardin resides in a mobile home park in the Monroe, Louisiana, area. We are to attempt to observe him possibly reading a newspaper, walking with or without a cane, using or not using a seeing-eye dog, or driving. He has been divorced several times, and we are to locate and contact his ex-wives and get their opinions of Mr. Bardin. We are to complete a background check as to prior lawsuits and

25

financial situation. We have unlimited funds, and we are to pull out all stops.

We began, as always, with the background check and determined that Mr. Bardin has good knowledge of which attorneys to contact, of filing lawsuits, and of winning. He is savvy in his ability to choose trial attorneys in personal injury cases. He has a history of damages cases in a several-parish area in Louisiana and also in Texas district courts. We also learned that he lives a high lifestyle on other people's money. We were able to locate his four ex-wives, who were then residing in Texas, Louisiana, and Florida, and who were more than happy to speak to us. Some of them even knew each other, having become acquainted after their respective marriages to Mr. Bardin broke up and even became good friends. Each described Mr. Bardin as a "real con artist." That was one of the first descriptions we got from each of these ladies, without any prompting. We asked each of them if they knew about his head injury and blinded condition, and each reported that they have nothing to do with him now and don't know where he is living or what he is doing, but they would be surprised if this were a legitimate claim.

After learning all we could about Mr. Bardin and obtaining several good photos of him from our attorney as well as the ex-wives, we set out to determine what he was up to now.

At this point, I must point out that my husband was still new in this business. He was constantly telling me that I was being overly cautious. Well, I would explain to him that being too careful is good because one can always repeat an attempt. On the other hand, if you go like a bull in a china shop, as he tended to do, you can't ever go back. I will grudgingly admit that his method worked this particular time.

The Plan: Don had what I thought a pretty lame idea. We had a dark blue Astro van at this time and had magnetic signs made for the side of the van. He wanted our signs to say "Nosliw Utilities," pronounced "Noslie" with a silent w. If it's not apparent, Nosliw is Wilson spelled backward. I thought then, and still do, that this was not the most brilliant choice for a company name, but I didn't want to argue as he was trying to contribute. Plus, he had been a car salesman for years and, as we all know, car salesmen can be very pushy.

His other, again lame in my opinion, idea was that we would go with our "Nosliw Utilities" magnet signs on either side of our van to attempt to observe our man. I would be in the back of the van with the camera. He would walk around the area "observing utility poles" and taking notes. If anyone asked what he was doing, he would simply tell them we had been retained by the parish to observe the utility poles to determine which poles needed to be replaced. I chose to go along, but hesitantly. We arrived at the park and located Mr. Bardin's lot. It appeared no one was at home. Therefore, Mr. Wilson got out his clipboard, legal pad, and pen and began walking around observing utility poles as we awaited the arrival of our claimant. Then he got another brilliant idea. I must admit, had I known what he was going to do, I'd have been not only sweating bullets in the back of that van in that ninety-five-degree summer heat, I would have also been a nervous wreck!

My husband walked up to a neighbor of Mr. Bardin, who was sitting outside his trailer. He gave his explanation of why we were there observing utility poles and then plunged in with, "You know, I think I know that guy that I saw leaving that lot over there, but I can't seem to recall his name!"

The neighbor said, "Oh, I know him and wave at him, but I don't know his name."

"What's he doing now?" Don Wilson asked.

"Oh, he works somewhere at a camp over at Toledo Bend as a fishing guide."

Well, Don just about had an accident on getting this critical piece of information, but he was able to continue with some mild conversation and told the guy he enjoyed talking to him. Knowing my husband, I assumed he'd forgotten that I was roasting in the back of that van while he was making a friend out of a stranger. I will have to say, though, that I quickly got over that once he got back to me and explained what information he'd just learned.

We continued with our pretext of telephone pole work and left for the day.

Toledo Bend's shoreline is about 1,250 miles. There are many fishing camps all along the area, some on the Louisiana side, and some on the Texas side. Our next step was to update our client, who was ecstatic, and then to try to get some kind of information as to the names of the fishing camps along the shoreline. On our way back, we drove along the borderline between Louisiana and Texas, and, with the Don Wilson luck, we pulled right into a rest stop that had a wonderful map of the entire shoreline with the location and names of all the fishing camps.

The next day we sat down in our office, and I started my research. This was before computers, or at least before we had any knowledge of them, when we used to call a central number and ask the person on the other line to look up a phone number. Through this method, I managed to get number after number of the various camps and must have contacted at least thirty of them. In each call, I would say that we had a party that wanted to hire a fishing guide by the name of Peter Bardin, who had been recommended by a friend. None of those contacted knew of Mr. Bardin, Fishing Guide. I was discouraged, tired of the telephone, and decided maybe Mr. Neighbor didn't know of what he spoke.

The next day, Don "Bull in a China Shop" Wilson said, "Let me give it a try."

"Sure," I said, "Go ahead, have at it and good luck!"

Again, with that Don Wilson luck, on the third call I heard him say, "Oh, yeah? He works from your camp. Wonderful. Let me get with my party, and we'll pick out a weekend and call you back."

As I sat there with my mouth hanging open, he explained that he had just spoken with the proprietor of the Fisherman's Dream camp, shown on our map in the northern Louisiana area. The proprietor said that Peter does work from his camp but only on weekends and not every weekend. He suggested that we call before we go to make sure Peter is working that weekend. Well, we were obviously beside ourselves when we contacted Walt. He said to go on up there, have a lovely weekend, and don't worry about costs.

Soon a weekend became available, and we confirmed that our man would be at the camp. We reserved a cabin, packed our bags, and drove on up with camera in hand. Again, "Bull" Wilson had another one of his plans. Well, he certainly had done well so far, so I said, "Let's go for it!"

The Plan: Don would be retired from a major oil company. He is the editor of a monthly paper for them, and each month they have been featuring Louisiana fishing spots. We want a guide to take us out at Toledo Bend so we can get some points of interest from our guide and take some video of the shoreline. I wondered why we needed video if we were doing a newspaper layout, but what do I know! We would pay the going rate for our guide, I would handle the video, trying to get Mr. Bardin in as much of the film as possible without him knowing, and Don would talk to him, asking questions and hoping to distract him and take photos of the shoreline with a still camera.

When we got there, we approached the proprietor explaining who we were and getting the key to our cabin. He said that Peter Bardin had not yet shown, but he was expected. He took us to our cabin and pointed out Peter's, saying we should watch for his burgundy Bronco. We hung out for the weekend, but old Peter never did show up. The proprietor, Roy Ball, was apologetic, saying that sometimes Peter does that, things come up, etc. We told him we would just try again. We called for the next weekend, and Roy reported that Peter Bardin had told him that his son had had a ball game, and that was why he didn't show. He said we would be there this coming weekend, so we reserved the same cabin and drove up there. Peter was a no-show once again.

The third time being the charm, we made our reservations and drove up to Fisherman's Dream campsite, which was now beginning to feel like home. As we walked into the "office, store, bar" area, Proprietor Ball welcomed us back with open arms, and we immediately spotted Peter Bardin from our photos at the bar area smoking and joking with some guys. Roy brought us over to Peter and introduced us, saying, "And here's your guide!"

We talked to Peter for a few minutes, asking what time he wanted to get started and explaining Don's "editor of the paper" story. I expected him to be at least a little suspicious, but he was not at all.

So, first meeting successful. We agreed on an hour on the water, and Peter said we would leave when convenient for us and that he was at our service. What a guy! We agreed to meet at 8 a.m. the following morning. The next morning, Pete was waiting for us when we arrived at the dock. With camera in hand, Pete helped me into the boat as any gentleman would, Don helped himself in, and off we started. I have to put in at this point that I am a real cheapskate. I had purchased some cheap tapes, and as I was checking the camera, something was wrong with the tape. It wasn't moving! Here was our big chance, and, because of my cheapness, we were blowing the whole case! I blurted out, "The camera is not working!"

The very calm and cool Pete said, "Well, do you have a spare tape in your car?" I didn't have a spare, but I had one that we'd taped another case on, and I sure was ready to tape over it to get this on film. I told him that I did, and he said, "Well, we'll go back and get it. You need to have good working equipment!"

I was pretty shocked at how accommodating he was. We went back, I got the other tape, checked the camera, and it whirled right along.

So, out we went. I started filming the shoreline and moving the camera around so to get our guide in the video. Don questioned him, took some stills, and I was able to pick up the conversation with the audio. We rode around the lake for almost an hour. Peter would point out, "See that guy over there in the red shirt? He always fishes right there. See that bottle floating out there? That's what they call Bottle Fishing."

We rode over to the Texas side, and Peter pointed, "Look over there, see that cabin third from the right? That's the cabin you all are staying in." It was soon apparent that Peter wasn't paying any attention or just did not care that he was being photographed, so I just put him in the picture most of the time. All he cared about was getting the $125.

When we got back to the dock, Peter helped me out of the boat, saying he hoped we got what we came out for. I told him we certainly did. He then said that we should come back out and do some fishing next time. I said I would only come back out to fish if he would put the bait on the hook for me. He assured me he would, and shook our hands with a big smile and a thank you. Don and I got into our van and took off down the road with the *Mission: Impossible* theme playing in our heads. After we submitted our final report and the videotape, Walt said that he'd just popped some popcorn and watched the best movie he'd ever seen.

Bull in a China Shop

We got this assignment right after our triumph with the blind fishing guide, in which Don was instrumental in the success of the case. So, he was all puffed up and ready to call the shots. He would generally want to go forward without really thinking the matter through. He would get an idea on the spur of the moment and just want to act upon it. He was continually telling me I was too cautious. People aren't suspicious. You don't have to be that careful. He was still new on the job, and I kept having to pull him back. I kept telling him that if you go with your first instinct and screw up the case, you can't go back and try again.

This assignment involved a man who had an auto repair place in downtown Monroe, Louisiana. He was on disability and admitted to running the shop but claimed he did not do any actual repair on the vehicles. He had employees who did that. He just supervised. We were to attempt to observe him and take video of him at his place of business or anywhere else, for that matter, performing activities contrary to his injuries.

We'd been discussing the case on the way to Monroe, and Don was patiently listening to my suggestions, lame though he thought they were. What I suggested

was that we first do our background check, locate the residence where Ben Hebert resided, check that out, and then locate Ben's garage downtown and check it out to see what we could see from across the street.

We did the background check, finding that Mr. Hebert had a bad history of insurance claims and also some substantial financial problems. We then went to his home and found no activity there. Don was very patient in doing all this boring stuff. We next headed to Ben's garage. When we got there, Don proceeded to pull directly into the entrance of the garage, located in a business area on a narrow street. I said, "What are you doing?"

He said, "Just let me do it my way for a change."

I knew this was a big mistake, but it was too late. Don "Bull in a China Shop" Wilson had done his thing. Mr. Hebert came up to the driver's side of the van. Don said, "We were just driving in from out of town and were having some trouble with our van and wanted to know if you'd take a look at it."

I thought I was going to have an attack. Mr. Hebert looked at him and then at me, obviously suspicious. "Why did you come into my shop? What kind of problem are you having? I can't just take you ahead of others. You'll have to wait or come back."

Finally, Don said that we'd come back, and we left. We were pretty much screwed.

We went back home to try and think of a way to salvage this disaster. With Hebert's experience in insurance fraud, he knew about P.I.s and about being watched. Now he had a good look at both of us. We finally decided to use our other car and think of a way to be in the area and unsuspected. There had recently been a lot of news coverage about how Congress was engaged in heated debates about doing away with the penny. So, we devised a plan to "Save the Penny." We made up hats for each of us and a sign for our car that said, "Save the Penny." We had cards made with "Save the Penny" on them, and I tediously glued five pennies on each of the cards.

We then proceeded back to Monroe and parked at the corner near Ben Hebert's garage. We took turns standing on the corner, giving out our "Save the Penny" cards to passersby, who all thought we had totally lost our minds. At one point, old Ben came up and asked us what the hell we were doing. I'm sure he recognized us. We left pretty quickly after that.

Don pretty much listened to me from then on, and we, as the song goes, "Did it my way."

Deer, Squirrel, and Bear

This case was requested by a nearby parish school board and their insurance carrier. They had a schoolteacher who was on workers' comp because of a work-related injury, and one of the school board members saw a picture of her in the local paper with a deer she had just shot. Talk about a red flag. So, they called Wilson & Wilson in hopes that we could get an idea of her activities either at home or, if possible, hunting deer. She was Alice Covington, residing in an outlying subdivision. A lot of attorneys and insurance adjusters assume that a P.I. can just park out by the claimant's house and get video of them doing yard work, home renovations, and the like. That is far from the case. Surveillance in that manner is almost always a failure.

We do always check out the residence first in the event there is a library or store across the street where we can park. Not so in this case. What we do next is a background check to determine if the claimant may be involved in other activities. Of course, in this case, we already knew that she was a deer hunter. An additional check provided information that she and her husband belonged to a hunting club located in Mississippi. There

are many such clubs in Mississippi, but in speaking with sources, we were able to determine the name and location of her club. It was north of the Louisiana/ Mississippi line.

In several of our cases we used pretexts. In the old days, one could do that. We cannot do that anymore as it is considered entrapment. It's unfortunate because it is so much fun to do. But I also understand why it's unacceptable, and a case can be thrown out in court if it is learned that such tactics were used. For this case, we had some cards printed up that we were with Channel 19 out of New Orleans, and we had a Channel 19 magnetic sign put on our camera. Again, I was the camera person and Don was the director. We were going to be doing a documentary on deer hunting.

Just before the holidays in the late 1980s, we proceeded to the deer camp. We chose to walk about and speak to a few of the club members. The first guy we talked to said we would have to get permission from the club president to do any filming. He referred us to "Bear" McBride, who had a permanent camp up here. He pointed out the house on the front of the property. Bear was not there, but we found out when he would be there and advised that we would come back at that time.

We did return and later knocked on their door, explaining to Bear what our intentions were. He asked us inside, and we all had coffee. After Don put his charm on Bear, we were pretty much "in like Flynn," but we were told that we would not be allowed to go into the woods and mingle with the hunters for safety purposes. That pretty much put a big hole in our efforts to video Alice Covington in action. The closest we could get was at the end of the actual campsite area. We would be able to film the hunters going in on their motorcycles and coming back with their kill.

We told Bear that at this time, we would just walk around and get the feel of the camp and the hunters, and he said we could make ourselves at home. The first thing we did was to locate the Covingtons' camp. The camps were laid out in rows, and the Covingtons' was the fifth camp from the entrance into the woods on the first row. We had gotten a description of their vehicles as well as a photo ID of Alice, so we were able to pick them out fairly quickly. Later that day, some of the hunters came back in, but Alice never left her camp.

We returned the next day, arriving at the time that the hunters would leave and began filming as they took off on their bikes or walked into the woods. Mr. Covington went out, but again Alice stayed behind. Later that day, we finally saw her leave her camp and spend some time with some of the other women. We overheard some of the members talking about how Alice had a pet squirrel that she had trained to run over her outstretched arms, going back and forth from one hand, around her neck, and over to the other arm. We asked her to perform for us, and we got this on tape. Several times the squirrel jumped or fell, and she had to get down on the ground and pick him up. One time it ran under the camp, and she had to get down and crawl under to retrieve the animal. This was negative to her alleged complaints, and thus helpful to our case.

Of course, we stayed around several days and got that same activity and more of the hunters, but Alice never did go out into the woods. On our last day, we spent some time with Mr. and Mrs. Bear as, by this time, we had become the best of friends. Bear informed us that he would like a copy of our filming. We weren't expecting this, but we later made a copy for him and edited out most of the squirrelly business. He told us

41

that they always hosted a dinner on New Year's Day, and he surely would be pleased if we would join them for the meal. It would be at 2 p.m., and all of the club members contribute food to the affair. We accepted the invitation and told Bear that we would like to end the documentary with that get-together.

On New Year's Day, we arrived early so we could visit with Mr. and Mrs. Bear. We went outside as the club members began going into the kitchen/dining room building, bringing in their turkey, casseroles, desserts, and many side dishes for a great feast. We were able to get video that included Alice Covington bringing in the turkey in one of those big Magnalite aluminum roasters.

So, in the end, we got some pretty good video of her activities even if she didn't get a deer. And we did enjoy our New Year's Day meal, sitting at the head table right next to Mr. and Mrs. Bear.

Deer Club President

We had another case involving deer hunting. We had been called in by a new attorney with the large law firm in New Orleans. His name was Michael Winston. He told us right up front that he did not want to use us. He'd had another investigating firm in mind that he'd been using, but the insurance company insisted that he use Wilson & Wilson. He also told us that he didn't expect that we could get the job done.

"I'm telling you right up front! I don't think you can do the job." Well, that was certainly a different way to start a relationship.

Our Assignment: They had a man on disability for the past ten years living in Montpelier, Louisiana. He had been a city employee. They were certain that he was faking his back injury because they'd heard he has bragged all over this small community that he was taking the insurance company. They had already sent several investigators to put him under surveillance. Several thought they had gotten him on film, but it turned out to be the claimant's brother. The claimant is Tim Williams, and his brother is Tom. There is only a year's difference in their ages, and they look a lot alike. No one has ever even gotten a look at this Tim guy.

We were to try to get video of him any way we could. He knows how to play the game, is very savvy, and is aware that they have been trying to nail him. We said we'd see what we could do and left Michael Winston with serious doubts. I will have to say, in his defense, he was very young. With more experience, I don't think he would have been quite so rude. But we had a big challenge, and one thing I love is a challenge. And with this attorney's attitude, we were going to get the job done no matter what.

The Plan: We first did our usual background on this subject, and in checking records, we learned that he and his wife are brand-new parents of a baby girl born just a month ago. We came up with another one of our foolproof plans. There was a well-known business across the country known as the "Welcome Wagon." Well, what's wrong with a "Welcome New Baby Wagon"? We would bring the new baby a bunch of baby items. We would contact the parents, tell them about our newly formed organization, and make an appointment to meet the parents, bring them some gifts, and even make a video of the event for a keepsake!

Our first stumbling block was the fact that they did not have a phone. The family lived way out in the country, so it would have caused immediate suspicion if we would have just shown up. We were, however, able to locate a neighbor who had a phone. We contacted the neighbor. In my best "Welcome New Baby Wagon" voice, I announced our purpose and that we were trying to get in touch with their neighbors, the Williamses. We understood they have a new baby, and we wanted to meet with them and bring some free gifts, but they don't have a phone. Our neighbor was thrilled to get Mr. Williams on the phone for us. We explained our intentions, and he was ecstatic and certainly would like to have us bring free goodies. He and his wife would love to have a video of the new baby. We agreed on a date and time.

Don and I went shopping at Wal-Mart. We bought a large laundry basket and filled it with diapers, baby food, talc, baby shampoo, some pink clothing, and a bunch of other baby stuff. We topped it off with a bottle of champagne for the parents and tied it up with cellophane and a pink bow and baby rattle. I must say, my talents in gift wrapping made it quite an attractive package!

Off we went to Montpelier, arriving at the appointed time. We had put our big basket, weighing about fifty pounds, in the trunk. Old Tim opened the trailer door before we even exited our vehicle. We explained to him that Don has a bad back and asked if he could please get the basket from the trunk for us. (Remember, Tim's disability is back problems.) He was more than happy to reach into the trunk and had no difficulty hauling the large basket out and up the five stairs and into his trailer. Of course, we explained that we wanted to begin the video right away, so we were able to get all that on film.

As we went into the trailer, I had the camera running and was able to make all the right moves by filming Mrs. Tim and their other children with close-ups of the new baby. As luck would have it, Tim had several deer heads mounted and hung from the walls. Well, we had to get video of those deer heads and, with audio on, questioned him about them. He proudly posed next to the heads and told us that he was the president of his deer-hunting club and has been for the past ten years. We got him to talk about that and asked about where the club hunted and the like. He explained that it was very near where we were and asked if we would like to

46

go out and take a look. I guess we would. We went out there with the camera rolling. He showed us several of the deer stands and even climbed up and down one of them for us! Marvelous!

We packed up our gear and advised that we would be mailing a copy of the tape of his little darling and his sweet family and wished him all the best. Of course, we completed our report and presented it along with the video to Mr. Winston. Our next conversation with him went something like this:

"Well, what can I say? I certainly owe you guys a big-time apology. I never thought you would have been able to do it! That is the absolute best video I've ever seen. I've sent a copy to the City of Montpelier and, of course, the insurance company, and I will never, quote me, never, use anyone but Wilson & Wilson again."

Mission: Impossible theme time again!

Kidnapping for The Colonel

I generally stay away from domestic cases. However, in this case, we got a call from Walter Broussard, our attorney in New Orleans. He had an uncle, The Colonel, living in Shreveport. The Colonel, as you may have guessed, was a retired army veteran. His son, Matt Archer, and his wife, Melissa Archer, had been divorced, and Matt had gotten domiciliary custody of The Colonel's six-year-old favored grandson, Matty. Melissa had visitation and was able to keep the child for several weeks during the summer months. At the time Walter was calling us, Melissa had the child and was refusing to return him to the father. Walter asked if we would give The Colonel a call and see if we could be of assistance.

As stated, we do not do domestic cases, but we were very fond of Walter and figured, what the heck, we could at least call grandpa. So, we did. True to his name, The Colonel was a gruff, no-holds-barred kind of ex-Army type and 75 years old. He told us that "that bitch" had his only grandson and was refusing to let his son, Matt, have him back. He asked if we would at least be willing to meet with him to talk the situation over

48

and see if we would agree to help. Money was no object. Well, when money is no object, it's kind of hard not to at least talk to the man!

The Colonel said he would be in Baton Rouge within the next few days. He and Matt met with us and said that they did not know where Melissa was living at this time. It was somewhere in either Livingston or Tangipahoa Parish. She has a boyfriend now. Her mother lives somewhere in the area, but she has moved to avoid Matt and grandpa. They think Melissa is probably living with her mother. They asked if we would at least try to find Melissa and little Matty. After that, we would notify Grandpa and Dad, and they would go collect the little tyke. This seemed like a reasonable request. It seemed like a relatively simple assignment, especially with my expertise in locating people. And, of course, with the "no object money" clause, what the heck! So, we gathered our information, and off we went. I contacted my "usual and confidential" sources of information and did locate Melissa's mother's new residence. We did some surveillance and neighborhood checking, but we could not find that Melissa was actually living at the residence. We continued our efforts in that regard and, of course, kept The Colonel abreast of our progress daily. Believe me, if I didn't call him, he sure called me!

Then one day, we were out checking out the mother's place when we saw a note on the front door. I discreetly approached the door and read, "Melissa, meet Uncle Billy at 850 Broad Street in Natalbany at 2 p.m. on Wednesday for the reading of the will." Wow, what a stroke of luck! This was a Friday. We called The Colonel, who was ecstatic, and we agreed that he and Matt would drive down to our fair city, and we would meet them at 10 a.m. on Wednesday at a nearby motel in Hammond, Louisiana.

At the appointed time and place, we knocked on room 206 and met with our clients. We discussed the case and had a map to Uncle Billy's address laid out for them. The Colonel said that he and Matt would take it from here; however, if we wanted to go with them, they would be obliged. We were hesitant since The Colonel was planning to wait for the arrival of Melissa and little Matty and attempt to grab the grandson and run. But we'd come this far, so what the heck? We might as well go for broke. A big mistake!

We still had our old blue Astro van. Don had had some foot surgery and was not able to drive, so I was the driver, Don was in the passenger seat, and The Colonel and Matt sat in the back seat. We planned to scout the neighborhood and locate the best place to park and await Melissa's arrival, then follow her to Uncle Billy's and, when she got out of her car with little Matty, The Colonel would jump out and grab the kid, get back in the van, and off we would go. Just like in the movies! Right? Wrong.

At 1 p.m. we drove over to the subdivision and parked under a lovely shade tree. The first thing we didn't expect: We saw the chief of police of the Town of Natalbany driving over to our surveillance location! I told them to follow my lead. That meant, "Colonel, shut up!" Chief Patterson exited his unit and approached this interesting foursome with, "How are you all this fine afternoon?"

"Just fine, Chief."

"I've had a complaint from one of the residents in this neighborhood that they observed you folks sitting here and were wondering what you were up to."

"Oh, of course, Chief. Understandable. Well, our daughter is engaged to this young man in the backseat here, and we are waiting for her to meet us. They are interested in a house that is for sale, and once she arrives, we are going to look at it."

"Oh, that's fine. Well, you have a nice afternoon." The Chief tipped his hat and parted.

Well, The Colonel was impressed with my ingenuity, and we all relaxed. A little too soon, I might add.

Not long after that, Matt spotted Melissa driving into the subdivision with little Matty. The Colonel shouted, "Oh, she's got that son-of-a-bitch boyfriend with her too!" We followed. Melissa pulled into the driveway, and I pulled in after her. She got out of her car along with little Matty and the boyfriend. The Colonel jumped—yes, all 75 years of him—out of the side door and ran over and tried to grab little Matty. Melissa was too quick for him, though, and grabbed her son's hand and hauled him into the house. In the meantime, the boyfriend ran over to The Colonel, who managed to give the boyfriend a pretty good right hook!

Someone must have called 911 because, during the fisticuffs, the same Chief of Police pulled up with sirens blasting and jumped from his unit. He had shaving soap on his chin and his barber's cape flying from his neck. Furious, he ran over to me and bellowed, "You lied to me! I want you all over at the station immediately! And I'm going to charge you," he said, pointing at me, "with obstruction of traffic and misrepresentation."

In the meantime, one of his officers had restrained The Colonel and The Boyfriend.

Well, what can I say? We drove over to the police station and, with tails tucked between our legs, we walked in. The Chief was so enraged that he was spitting his words out! And there was Melissa, little Matty, and The Boyfriend, who all looked incredibly triumphant, which really pissed us off. After all, we were the good guys! We tried to explain this to The Chief, who just couldn't get past the fact that I had lied to him.

"Do we get our one phone call?" I asked. He reluctantly let me have a phone—no cell phones in those days.

It was a good thing I had Walter Broussard's phone number handy. I interrupted his dinner. Tough!

"Walter, we have a real problem here."

He said he didn't doubt it, knowing how his uncle is. He did explain it all to The Chief, who had no choice but to let us all go. He told The Colonel, Matt, Melissa, and The Boyfriend to all be back in the morning. To me, he said, "And you, if you ever show up in Natalbany again, I'll see that you are escorted out!"

I still think he was just mad because we had gotten one over on him. Well, actually, two over on him!

Some stories have a happy ending. Don and I were just glad to get home and have something to eat. The next day we got a call from The Colonel, who was ecstatic! He and Matt had gotten little Matty back, and they were on their way back to Shreveport. They wanted to stop by our place and let us formally meet the little guy. Well, sure, of course. Later that morning, they arrived. After they left, Don and I agreed that The Colonel was not the winner after all. That little brat ran all through our place, running after our cats, scaring them to death, marking the walls, and knocking stuff off the shelves and walls. It was the worst fifteen minutes of celebration in the history of Wilson & Wilson! But. Our client, The Colonel, was so happy to have his little guy back, even if he was the worst brat since Dennis the Menace!

Wilson & Wilson rule No 36. No more kidnapping capers.

BBQ Shrimp on The Gulf

This case occurred before Wilson & Wilson was even a thought when I was working for another small investigation firm. Their client was an attorney who really liked my work and had requested my services many times. This case involved a female who had been involved in a car crash with an eighteen-wheeler. Our client was the defendant trucking company. Our attorney was Bob Cockerham. He was aware that the plaintiff, Cathy Wilkerson, was a hairdresser who owned a beauty shop. She alleged that she ran the shop but didn't do hair anymore. In the accident, she had broken her foot.

My Assignment: Bob wanted me to go to the shop and get my hair done, the works, as much as I could get so I could be there and observe Cathy for as long as possible. So, I called and made an appointment using a false name. My fake name all these years, by the way, has been Marion Moore. I had no problem getting an appointment with Cathy, so I called Bob and told him we were over the first hill.

I got to the shop early, hoping to get a look at Cathy. She was already doing someone's hair. The foot she had broken was her right. She stood the entire time and used that foot to pump the chair up and down with no problem. She walked just fine, and, as they say in insurance jargon, appeared to have no difficulty walking, having no limp, and did not use a walking aid.

My turn. I asked for a haircut, color, and perm. She went through the entire process, and I was there for about three hours. While I was in the chair, Cathy got a phone call. She told the girl that answered the phone to take a number. The answerer of the phone said, "But, Cathy, it's your attorney."

"Oh," she said to me, "it's my attorney, so I'd better take it if you don't mind?"

I said, "Oh, no, go ahead and take your time." I strained as much as I could to listen. She was discussing her case and the prospective court date for trial, which was two days away. The only thing I heard well was that she told him she would not accept the $40,000 offered. And she laughed a lot.

After she got off the phone, she started telling me about the accident she'd had and her broken foot. She and the girls were all laughing it up and having a good old time at the expense of my client! She even told me that she had been offered a measly $40,000, but she wasn't going to accept it. She wanted at least twice that. Then she told the girls, "And when I get my settlement, we're all going to the Gulf Coast for BBQ shrimp!"

Yuk, yuk!

And the whole time she was working on me, she pumped the heck out of my chair with that broken right foot.

I couldn't wait to call Bob. I found the nearest payphone I could—no cells in those days. I told him everything that had happened, especially about the phone conversation with her attorney and the prospective trip to The Gulf Coast with the whole gang for BBQ shrimp. Bob was ecstatic. "By the way, how does your hair look?" he asked.

"I look like Little Orphan Annie"! I said. And I did.

He told me that since we had set Cathy up, I would not be able to testify. However, he wanted me to be in the courtroom by 8:30 a.m. on Monday. The trial started at 9 a.m. He told me just to walk in and sit way in the back. Don't say anything to him or anyone else.

I was looking forward to Monday. I did my best to make sure my hair looked exactly like it did when I left Cathy's shop, which was pretty easy since it really did look like the Orphan. I walked into the courtroom and noted that Cathy and her attorney were yukking it up in the front. Right after I settled down on the last bench, Cathy did a casual look around, saw me, and then did a perfect Three Stooges double take! The next thing I knew, she and her attorney, along with several other people, disappeared into the judge's chambers behind the courtroom. I saw Bob walk in, and he barely glanced in my direction and was signaled to join the group in the chambers.

In about ten minutes, Bob came out and said to me, "Guess what? They settled for $40,000. Oh, and I'll pay to get your hair fixed."

Lost Cat

Doing surveillance is difficult. As I've said before, a P.I. can't just sit out in front of the subject's home without causing suspicion. There you are in a strange neighborhood, and people notice cars that are not familiar, especially with someone sitting in that car. You can try sitting in the backseat or in the back of a van, but the vehicle is still out of place. So, one of the ploys we have used is getting a picture of a dog or cat and going about a neighborhood door to door around where the subject resides and showing that picture to the residents, telling them we have lost the animal and asking if they have seen it. That gives you some time in the area to, hopefully, observe your subject.

In this particular case, we had learned that our disabled subject was a mechanic by trade and worked on vehicles at his residence. This neighborhood was a typical subdivision of a middle-class nature. We decided to drive around the area until we could see that the subject was working on cars or trucks in his yard. One day we were there and, bingo, he was out there working under the hood of a truck. We parked down the street with the rear of the van toward our subject.

As this was a number of years ago, when I was still kind of cute, I put on my shorts and got a photo of our brindle-colored cat, actually named Brindle.

Don stayed in the van with the video camera. I stepped out and began knocking on doors while Don was busy filming.

As I knocked on each door, I tried to spend as much time talking to the resident as possible to give Don more time to film. After going to several houses, I knocked on the door of an older gentleman. I gave him my rehearsed speech, "Good morning! My husband and I were driving around the other day with our cat in our van, and she got out and ran off. I'm checking with some of you kind folks and asking if you may have seen this cat anywhere around?"

Then I showed the photo to the gentleman. He took the picture and looked it over and then shook his head, saying that he had not seen my cat. He asked if he could have my name and telephone number in case he did see the cat, as he would be glad to give me a call. I chose to provide him with my correct name and telephone number, and we talked for several minutes. As I was expressing my thanks and appreciation, he continued the conversation, asked me inside, would I like some water or anything at all. I declined and finally was able to move on to the next house.

We spent some more time in the neighborhood, and we did get some pretty good video of our subject working on several vehicles.

That evening as we were turning in for the night, the phone rang. It was Walter Williams. "Do you remember me? You asked if I had seen your cat?"

"Oh, yes, I remember you."

He said, "Well, I found your cat!"

Well, of course, we had not really lost a cat, so we knew he hadn't actually found her. I explained, "Oh, well, thanks for calling, but we did find her. In fact, she's right here now."

He said, "Oh, no, I've found your cat, and she's right back here in the woods behind my house."

"Oh, Mr. Williams, I appreciate your help and concern, but really, we've found our cat, and thank you very much. Good night."

The next day we got another call from Mr. Williams. "Mrs. Wilson, I know you said you found your cat, but I'm sure it's her I've seen in the back of my house. She looks just like the picture you showed me."

"No, no, Mr. Williams. We have our cat right here."

He said, "Where did you find her? Are you sure it's your cat?"

"We contacted a vet's office near your area, and someone had found her and brought her there," I lied.

He insisted, "I'm sure this is your cat. Would you come back out here and take a look?"

"I appreciate your interest, but we know we have our cat." He kept persisting, but I finally was able to hang up the phone. By now, Don is laughing hysterically, "You know he's in love! He hasn't found any cat. He just wants you to come back out there!"

I told him he was nuts. But, do you know, I continued to get calls from old Mr. Williams for the next two weeks, still insisting that he'd found my cat.

Speaking of Cats

I had forgotten about this case until I got another call from this client in the midst of writing this book. When I get a call from her, I always ask myself, "Are you sure, Nancy, that you want to call this woman back?" And I generally do, as she is one of the few non-insurance or non-attorney clients that actually pays.

About fifteen years ago, a mutual acquaintance referred me to this client. The client, Betty, had her own business, and she needed someone to run background checks on prospective employees. It sounded simple enough. We met and agreed on conditions. I did a few of these background checks for her, and she paid. The next time was a background check on a prospective partner to whom she was considering going into business, who turned out to be a prospective boyfriend. Well, that's okay. I took the case, and she paid.

When Betty called this time, she explained that she wanted me to help find her cat, knowing I had several cats and was a big-time cat lover. It seems she was divorcing her husband, and they were having a cat custody squabble. Betty had taken all of her cats into her apartment, except for one, Starlight. Starlight had a twin, Starbright. Well,

Starbright and Betty were pining for Starlight, but Mr. Ex-Husband, who was abusive to Starlight, would not let Betty have her. "If he doesn't like her, why won't he let you have her?" I asked in all sincerity.

"Because he doesn't want me to have her. He wants to be cruel and mean!" she said.

"Why don't you just go get her?" I asked.

"He'll know I have her," she said. This was getting us nowhere.

My Assignment: Betty was going to get the cat from Mr. Ex-Husband's house when he was gone. She wanted to know the name of my vet, and she would board Starlight with him for "a couple of months." She would then place signs around the former marital domiciliary reading, "REWARD! $888.88!" The signs would describe Starlight and include her telephone number.

Of course, I asked, "Why $888.88? Why not $800? Or $500? Or $1,000?"

"Oh, he won't believe it's me if I don't say $888.88!" Since I didn't want her to go into one of her twenty-minute explanations, I just let it go.

Her next move was to let her ex know that she had hired me to find the cat who was, by now, getting my utmost sympathy. After the two months, I was to call her and tell her I'd found the cat. (She was clear that I would have to actually make this call to her in case the Ex had tapped her phone!). And she would then pick her up.

During the two months the cat was in hiding, I had reason to visit my vet, with whom I was good friends. He asked, "What about this Betty person?" "Your guess is as good as mine," I responded.

"I think she's a nut!" he replied.

"Join the club!" I said. "But she's good for the money," I promised, "so we'll both come out okay." When I explained the rest of the case, he just shook his head and shrugged.

After two months, we met at a super-secret spot, and we agreed I would make "the phone call" announcing that I'd found Starlight. I was then to go to my vet and take Starlight, bring her to my house, and Betty would come over to get her. By the way, she was an adorable cat. I was thinking about telling Betty she'd gotten away and keeping her myself. Betty arrived. She wrote out a check for $888.88. My instructions were to cash the check, deduct my fee from the amount, and give the balance back to Betty.

I followed those instructions and vowed that I would never, ever, take another case from this woman. But I did, unfortunately. And that's another story.

The Broken Ankle Hopper

This case involved surveillance once again. Well, it was time for some more Wilson & Wilson ingenuity. Our subject lived in a small town in Albany, Louisiana. He had a "slip and fall" in a grocery store and had broken his ankle.

Our Assignment: We are to attempt to get video of the subject performing activities contrary to his alleged injuries.

On our first trip to Albany, we located our subject's home, situated in a typical subdivision. It was on a small and narrow road, and the houses were pretty close together. There was not much of a shoulder to even think about parking. We did a background check on him to see if he was working, see if he had any hobbies such as golf or tennis, and find out if he belonged to a health club. No, none of that.

In many of these cases, I contact neighbors, generally by telephone, and engage them in a conversation, hopefully getting them talking and telling us something useful. Sometimes I luck up and find someone who hates the guy. That is the ultimate win. In this case, we found just that someone, a neighbor who lived just to the right of our subject. This neighbor told us that he had nothing good to say about our subject because he was on disability and claimed to have a broken ankle, but yet he sees him working in his yard and has even seen him digging holes. "Now, how can you dig with a shovel with a broken ankle?" he expressed in anger.

At this point, we were able to level with our informant, so he told us, "You can drive by almost every day in good weather and see him outside doing something." This was fabulous news, but with the layout of the neighborhood, we still could not establish surveillance anywhere. So, in the days that followed, we would drive down the street in front of our subject's house.

Don was driving, and I was operating the camera from the back of the van. One time we drove by and, sure enough, he was digging a post hole for a fence. We were able to get video of him over several days as he put up the fence. Another time he was mowing his lawn. Another time he was edging. The best of all, and the icing on the cake, was the time he was washing his RV. It looked like he was going to be busy for a while, so we did the block, and he was still at it. We did the block again, and he was standing on top of his RV still washing. Around the block again and he was still on the top of his RV. Just then, he hopped, yes, I said he hopped, from the roof of the RV to the roof of his house! And, as we'd made the block again, we got him jumping from his house roof back to the roof of the RV! It was fabulous.

We sent our report and the video to our customer, after which we got a call from the adjuster who said, "That is the absolute best video we have ever seen!"

Some months after, we got another call from our adjuster, saying they were going to trial in New York. They flew me over there as a witness. I was sworn in, and then they played the video. Sometimes video is of just one day's activities negative to the injury, and the claimant will try saying, "Oh, I was having a good day that day." In this case, the claimant sure couldn't say that since our video was taken over a ten-day period and, of course, had that fabulous ending.

It's fun to be the star witness.

Wal-Mart Pusher

I got this assignment after Don had passed away. I didn't like surveillances when there was the two of us. I really didn't like them now that I was by myself!

Our subject in this case was a young twenty-one-year-old male. He was living at home and going to college. My client said that he plays basketball, having a hoop at home. He also works at Wal-Mart—but in his deposition he claims to be a department manager, which requires little activity. He had hurt his back in a car crash. My job: Try to get some video of him shooting hoops or performing any activity negative to his injuries.

I first drove out to his house and spotted the basketball hoop right out in front of the residence. I drove by a few times but never did see him out there. So, I decided to go to the local Wal-Mart store and see what he does there. Of course, I sure couldn't walk around the store with a video camera. I was hoping against hope that maybe he'd be working near the camera department. I could shop for cameras, and under the guise of comparing them to my "old" camera, use mine to get pictures. Yeah, right, in my dreams! Well, stranger things have happened.

Our subject's name was Sam Boudreaux. I got a photo ID of him and saw that he was a good-looking young man with brown hair, six-foot-two, tall and slim. I knew that Wal-Mart employees wear name tags, so that was certainly helpful. On my first day at the store, I was able to spot Sam. He had his red Wal-Mart vest on with "Sam" right there on his name tag. This first time he was walking around the store chatting with co-workers. He was nowhere near the camera department. Darn it.

The next day I went back. I have to tell you that I got to know every inch of that Wal-Mart. I did all my shopping there and sometimes several times daily. Several times I found that Sam was working as a cashier. That was great! He would fill up those plastic bags and then hoist them into the shopping cart. Too bad I couldn't pull out my camera. Too bad the camera department in all Wal-Marts, including this one, is way in the back of the store. Well, at least I saw what he was doing and could testify to it.

Several times I'd get tired of shopping and would go out and sit in my little red Grand Prix. One day I was sitting there, and I saw Sam come out onto the parking lot. He started stacking carts! Now the Wal-Mart stores have those motorized push-cart things that push the stacks of carts along, but at that time, the cart crew would stack them and physically push the whole lot of them over to the store. This day I sat in wonderment and joy as he stacked twenty to thirty carts and pushed them across the parking lot. I don't know how much a thirty-cart row would weigh, but it sure would be tough to do with a bum back!

I grabbed my camera and went from the front seat to the backseat and back again, getting Sam on film performing this activity several times that day. I went back the next day and several days after that, wrestling around in my little red Grand Prix, turning myself into a sixty-year-old pretzel, but I got some great video. One time he headed straight to my car and went right in front of the window while I was in the backseat. I continued to video and didn't skip a beat. Nothing could stop me now.

Most of the time, I don't hear of the outcome of my cases and, sad to say, this was one of those times. But I would suspect that they probably showed the plaintiff attorney the video and settled out of court.

STATEMENTS

Nancy Wilson in the '80s, the decade she founded the firm.

Drunk & Disabled

This case was also in my novice days in this business while working for one of my all-time favorite supervisors, Earl Webster. This was a continuing disability case and was a straightforward assignment. The investigator is to speak to at least three sources, generally neighbors, plus an interview with the claimant. In the meeting, you took a written statement. This was before recorded statements, so I'm dating myself. We used a three-sheet lined form with carbon paper between the sheets. For those born much later than me, I think you can look up carbon paper in a dictionary or on the web!

After hand-writing the statement, one has the claimant sign the statement, the investigator witnesses it and gives the last copy to the claimant. The original is mailed with the report to the client, and the second is kept in the file.

The claimant in this case was a gentleman in his sixties, Joe Kiersey, a local resident suffering from a back problem. His address was in a lower-class neighborhood. I drove to his residence, parked in the driveway, got out of the car, and knocked on the door. This was in the early '70s, in the first age of the miniskirt, one of which I was wearing. Old Joe came to the door wearing just his briefs. Not boxers, briefs. Well, to say the least, I was taken aback. I was also one of the first females in this business, and I wasn't about to let this stop me! Would a man let this keep him from his duty? No! So I proceeded onward.

"Mr. Kiersey, my name is Nancy Champagne. I'm representing ABC Insurance Company. I need to obtain a written statement from you concerning your disability." (Champagne was my last name before I married Don.)

Old Joe said that would be fine, but perhaps it would be a good idea if he put some pants on. I agreed that it would be a good idea. He left and returned with khakis on and opened the door. His residence was a one-room apartment. To the left were a double bed and a nightstand, and to the right, next to the door was a small sofa. As I entered, he announced that he had "been drinking." Since I had now grown a pair of gonads, this did not affect me, no, not me. I just said, "That's okay." Or something equally brilliant.

I sat on the sofa as close to the door as I could squeeze myself. Joe sat on the bed. As soon as he sat down, he picked up a fifth containing a clear liquid that was probably vodka or gin and upped the bottle to his lips, taking in a hefty slug. Being a gentleman, he asked if I'd care for a drink. Since I was on duty, I declined. I began taking down his statement. We start by identifying the claimant by full name, address, date of birth. By this time, I'd decided to make this the shortest statement in the history of written statements. I recorded a total of five sentences. I was going into the last sentence, "Everything in this statement is correct and true to the best of my knowledge, and I have received a copy of the same."

Then I stood up and started across the room and was telling him that he needed to sign the statement. He took the clipboard from me, and I handed him my pen. He drew a shaky "J" and then said to me, "Would you do me a favor?"

"Sure," I said, thinking he wanted a glass of water or something. Not hardly.

He said, "Can I kiss your butt?"

"Noooooooooooooooo," I said. I reached over to grab the clipboard, always faithful to duty, but he grabbed it and moved it to the back of the bed.

Then he said, "I'm sorry." So I reached behind him, grabbed the clipboard, grabbed my keys from my purse, hit the door, ran to the car, and, somehow, I managed to get the door open and start the vehicle. I was shaking and drove directly to Don's workplace. I got out of the car and ran through the showroom to his office. He asked what was wrong. I told him what happened, and he laughed! He thought the whole experience was just plain hysterical! So much for sympathy! I was reconsidering my upcoming marriage to him.

I was in no shape to work, so I went to my office. As soon as I got there, Earl asked what in the world was wrong. I sat across his desk and poured out my story. He just shook his head and said, "Champy, rule No. 42. When the guy comes to the door in his underwear, you don't go in!" So much for sympathy!

A few days later, I was telling of my horrific experience to the other female investigator, and she said, "Oh, I had him last year and went to the neighbor's first. They told me that Joe is a drunk, stays in that apartment all of the time, and has his liquor delivered. Oh, and he also invites the local young teen boys over to watch porn movies. Needless to say, I didn't enter his place."

Some of us are a whole lot smarter than others.

House for Sale in Mandeville

One of my favorite old lawyers in Hammond, Louisiana, Clyde Pitts, hired us for this case in which the claimant was Stephanie Flanders, a thirtyish mother and housewife. Her husband was a very successful businessman in the New Orleans area. A lot of the wealthy types from New Orleans reside across Lake Pontchartrain in the Mandeville/Madisonville area, where there are many beautiful upper-class subdivisions with homes in the high six figures. In the early 1990s, that was a lot of money.

Mr. Pitts called us in to discuss this assignment. It was going to be one of those in which we needed to use our best ingenuity. Ms. Flanders had been in an auto accident and was claiming debilitating injuries that prevented her from driving, doing her usual social club activities, shopping, and housework. She had to hire a housekeeper to take care of the house and had to depend on the housekeeper and her husband to take care of the kids and get them off to school. She allegedly spent almost all of her time at home and most of that time at bed rest.

Between our conversations with Mr. Pitts and our background check, we learned that she had never worked outside of the home, spent her time being Mr. Executive's wife, and hired lawn care workers and help inside the home. She wasn't a golfer or a tennis player. She had no outside activities. She and her husband belonged to the country club, but she wasn't active since her accident, which wasn't unexpected, as in many cases like this, the plaintiff lawyers caution their clients to tone down their activities.

As I've stated, one cannot just sit out in front of the house and expect not to be noticed, especially in a plush area like this one. The neighbors would have the police on us in a New York second. Our first drive through the neighborhood, however, provided us with a possible plan. There was a "For Sale" sign in front of the house! Bingo! We were going house-hunting! Of course, the home was listed with one of the better real estate agencies, and the agent was Mary Bender. We knew that when an agent shows a house, they generally ask the owners to be scarce. They prefer to show the homes without them there. But, we thought, if Stephanie was so bedridden, perhaps she'd be there, and we'd get a look at her.

We called Mary Bender and set up an appointment for Sunday at 2 p.m. We spruced up our van and ourselves, putting on our most expensive-looking casuals so that we'd look like we could afford a house priced in the six-figure range, and off we went. Mary met us at the door, and we learned immediately that disabled Ms. Flanders was not at home. We said we were sorry because we had a few questions for the owner. Not a problem, she told us, Mr. Flanders was outside by the pool!

Well, we toured the house, which was gorgeous, and I'd have given a few years of my life to have that house. We conferred with Mr. Flanders outside. He was, by the way, a really nice guy. I don't like deceiving the nice ones, but we had a job to do. We hung around as long as we could in case Stephanie would show up, to no avail. We reported our results to Mr. P, who said we'd had an excellent idea. Too bad it hadn't worked. But we were not through yet. We came up with a plan.

During the following week, we returned to the Flanders residence with measuring tools in hand and a tape recorder in my purse. For this act, we decided it would look better if Don remained in our vehicle. I knocked on the door, praying Ms. Flanders would be at home, and turned on the tape recorder. Petite Ms. Flanders answered the door, and I told her I was the lady who had looked at her house this past Sunday. I hated to bother her, but I wanted to measure an area in the kitchen. We had two refrigerators, and I wanted to see if they would fit side by side along that wall in there.

"Oh, sure," she graciously said, "come on in, but excuse my appearance, I've been polishing the doorknobs!" I was wondering what happened to the housekeeper! She was more than happy to let me measure anything I wanted as she bent over to clean up some cereal that had spilled on the kitchen floor. After we got through measuring, I asked if I could have another look through the house, and she was more than happy to lead me through the house as she flitted here and there and bounced up the stairs. I also have to say that she was a sweet young lady. I thought she probably had a lawyer who promised they could take my insurance company to the cleaners. The next day we reported the results to Mr. Pitts, who was ecstatic.

Sometime later, I got a subpoena to be deposed at Mr. Pitts' office by John Atchley, attorney for Stephanie Flanders. Mr. Pitts called, asking that I get there an hour or so before the deposition. We talked, and he advised. He said to answer each question as honestly as I possibly could. And under no circumstances was I to lie. I assured him I could handle it. At 1 p.m., gathered around the conference table sat Mr. Pitts, Mr. Atchley, the court recorder, and me.

Mr. Atchley had the floor and the most unpleasant, smug look on his face. He was ready for this lady P.I. Well, the lady P.I. was ready for him!

He started with softball questions: name, how long in business, where from, schooling, had I gone to "Private Eye" school (which I had not) and the like. He was so pleased that I was self-taught and was in business for myself as opposed to working for a big, well-known company. Then he got to the nitty-gritty of the deposition.

Atchley: "Have you ever seen Stephanie Flanders?"

Nancy: "Yes, I have."

Atchley: "Where did you see her?" Nancy: "At her house."

Atchley: "Was she in her yard?" Nancy: "No, she was inside the house."

Atchley, smugly: "Oh, I guess you were looking through her window."

Nancy: "No. I don't look through people's windows. I was inside her house."

Atchley, astonished: "How did you get into the house?!"

Nancy: "Ms. Flanders let me in through the front door."

Atchley, more astonished: "She let you in through the door herself? Why would she do that!?"

Nancy: "I told her I was the lady who'd looked at her house the other day, and now I wanted to measure the kitchen."

Atchley, smug again: "Oh, so you lied."

Nancy: "No, I didn't lie. I had looked at the house that past Sunday."

Atchley, still smug: "But you weren't really looking to buy a house."

Nancy: "Oh, yes! We've been looking for a house for the past several months."

Atchley: "But you live in Baton Rouge, so you certainly wouldn't be looking in Madisonville."

Nancy: "Of course we would. We've been wanting to move out of the city and have been looking in St. Francisville, Clinton, Folsom, Mandeville, and Madisonville."

Atchley: "But you wouldn't be interested in the Flanders house."

Nancy: "We absolutely would, if the price was right."

Mr. Atchley started packing up his briefcase, saying he had no further questions.

Later, back in his office, Mr. Pitts said I had done perfectly. And I told him that Don and I had been house-hunting for the past several months! In the parking lot, we were getting into our vehicle, and Mr. Atchley was getting into his two cars down. I waved, "Nice meeting you, Mr. Atchley!"

He was furious and red-faced. He just glared at me, didn't say a word, got in his car. I believe there are still burnt rubber marks on Mr. Pitts' asphalt!

All's Fair in Love and Nakedness

Among my duties are serving subpoenas and petitions and getting affidavits signed. In this case, we had a young twenty-six-year-old white male who was involved in an auto accident while driving someone else's vehicle. My attorney, Bobby Rinaldi, had determined that he had not had any auto insurance coverage of his own at the time of the accident. They had mailed the affidavit to him explaining the whats, whys, and wherefores, but got no response.

My job: To find this guy and get him to sign the affidavit. Simple. Not really.

My favorite thing in my work is locating people. And I'm pretty good at it. I have a 97 percent success rate. Yes, I am bragging. One of my customers used to say, "Get Nancy. She digs them up from the grave!"

Kyle Kieffer is from redneck country in the Livingston/Tangipahoa Parish areas of Louisiana. The address we had was his mother's address in Livingston. It is very common for young people to use their parents' address as their permanent address on driver's licenses, voter registration, and the like. It is also very common that the parents don't know where they actually reside, or if they do, they won't say. In this case, mama didn't know. So, I went about contacting my "usual and confidential" sources of information to locate this guy. I ultimately determined that he was recently married and that his bride was Pamela Murray of Ponchatoula, Louisiana. I pulled their marriage license application and noted the actual address and made a note of their bridesmaid, Sylvia Anthony, and best man, George Henry, should they be of assistance in this regard. I might need to contact them to see if they knew where our subject was.

I next proceeded to Pamela's parents' home in Ponchatoula, finding that she and her new husband are residing with her parents. She is at home. He is not. I explained to Pamela what is involved here, sharing that Kyle will be dismissed from the lawsuit if he will simply sign this affidavit that he had no insurance coverage at the time of the accident, and this will be to his benefit. She tells me that he is a truck driver and is "on the road," but he will be back home the day after tomorrow. I returned the day after tomorrow, and Kyle has not shown up yet.

We continued to play this game for the next week when I learned from Pamela's mom that Kyle sometimes stays at his trailer in Loranger between trucking jobs. No, she doesn't know where in Loranger the trailer is located. But he lives in a trailer park. So much for wedded bliss. So, off I go to try and find Kyle's home away from home. I check my "usual and confidentials" again to no avail. I next went to Loranger, which is a tiny rural area deep in the heart of redneck country, figuring there can't be that many trailer parks there. I did luck up and located a reasonably good-sized one right off the main highway traveling to Loranger.

My experience has been that landlords generally protect their tenants and are extremely reluctant to give out any information about them, especially where they live. In this case, however, my luck was holding. Ms. Duval, the owner and manager of the mobile home park, did not like Kyle for some reason. I did not ask why. I just bathed in my good fortune. She told me he lives on lot No. 17. I went there and knocked on the door, getting no response. As I was leaving, Ms. Duval stopped me and said that when he leaves for work, he is generally up at 5 a.m., when she sees his light go on, but he is gone by 5:15 a.m. If I could get there right at 5 a.m., I should be able to catch him.

Well, by now, I'd spent about two weeks trying to find this guy, and I was not going to fail. So, the next morning I left at 3 a.m. and drove over to Loranger. I arrived at Lot 17 at 4:45 a.m. There was a truck parked there that had not been there before, and no lights were on. Right at 5 a.m., a light flipped on inside, so I approached the door and knocked. A young white male opened the door. I said, "Are you Kyle Kieffer? He said, "No, I'm not." Well, my heart sank, but before it went all the way down, he said, "He's not here right now. He's in that trailer over there," and he pointed three trailers over. He also said, "He's probably sleeping."

By now, do you think I cared if he was sleeping? I drove over to the appointed trailer and knocked on the door several times, good and loud. A white female opened the door. She told me she was Sylvia Anthony—the bridesmaid, no less! I asked if Kyle Kieffer was there. She said he was asleep. I told her I needed to meet with him and why. She asked me in and pointed to a sofa right by the door. She said, "There he is?"

And there was Kyle, sound asleep on his stomach on the sofa. He had a sheet covering him to his waist and was shirtless. I woke him, and he turned toward me, yawning and rubbing his eyes. I told him that he needed to sign an affidavit that he had not had any car insurance at the time of that old accident. He said, "Oh, okay." He turned toward me, slipping off the covering. He was stark naked! He rose to a sitting position as I shoved a coffee table toward him and put the affidavit and a pen right in front of him. He did have the courtesy to pull the sheet over his lower body half. He signed, I grabbed pen and paper and was out of there.

Later that morning at 8 a.m., while I was on my way back to Baton Rouge, I called my attorney, Bobby Rinaldi, and told him that I had finally gotten that nasty old affidavit signed. I also asked, "Bobby, if the subject in question is naked, do I get hazard pay?"

He said, "Well, was he good looking or not?

"He was a twenty-six-year-old stud!"

"Then, no!"

Wives & Girlfriends

One of the things I learned in my early years as a lady P.I. was that ex-wives and ex-girlfriends are excellent sources of information. Especially in bad break-ups, they just hate those rotten SOBs so badly that they can't wait to help us out if we contact them. However, there are exceptions.

I had a case where we needed to get a look at a fellow here in Baton Rouge, Gary Masson. He was claiming a bad back from an auto accident, but the insurance company was suspicious, so they gave us a call. I checked him out and didn't find out a whole lot. He had a small claim history but no financial problems. He owned his home in a better-class neighborhood. I went out to the residence several times, and there was no sign that he was ever at home. He was no longer working. I had spoken to several neighbors. No one knew where he was, and no one had seen him in a long time. One of the neighbors said they knew he had a camp, but they didn't know where it was.

During the background check, I did find a divorce about a year before. In reading the file, I was hoping it would have a community property settlement that might say where the camp was. No such luck. It did turn out that the divorce was pretty nasty, and there was a continuing fight over child support. There was still some litigation going on in that regard. Since I'd always had luck in speaking with ex-wives in nasty divorce cases before, I had no problem calling on the ex-Mrs. Masson. I was able to reach her right away. In the past, as soon as I would get the ex on the phone, they would immediately start telling me tales of how rotten the SOB was and, boy, would she love for me to nail his ass, and so on and so on.

In this case, Mrs. Masson was pretty evasive. She said she would have to call me back, and I gave her my number. I was somewhat puzzled and a little concerned. The next day I got a call from Mr. Masson's attorney, Randy Breckenridge, one of the best-known ambulance chasers in the area. He got all over my case about what was I doing trying to find out information about his client and that I'd better call off the troops or he'd have my head. He called me several times with these threats.

On top of that, one morning, I was entertaining my insurance salesman at my house. As we concluded our business, and he was leaving via the front door, I saw a man who I immediately knew was Gary Masson. He had parked his pickup truck at the end of my driveway. He was out of his vehicle with a big, black Doberman on a leash. He asked me if l was Nancy Wilson and began to tell me who he was. I told him I knew exactly who he was and that he was to leave my property and that any conversation we would have would be our attorney speaking to his attorney. He stood there for a while with a sickly grin on his face, making gestures as though he was going to let the dog loose. He did get back in his truck shortly after that, however.

I was never able to do much with this case. It's too bad I was unprepared that day. I could have gotten great video out of the whole episode. So now, I'm very careful about talking to ex-wives and girlfriends.

Where the Buffalo Roam

I knew when I checked my voice messages on this case that it would have to go into this book. The message said, "Nancy, this is Ashley. I need you to find a buffalo!" When I called her back, I said, "You need me to find a what?" She said, "I knew that would get your attention!"

It seems the plaintiff in this case was driving down a country road in small-town Norwood, Louisiana when he struck a buffalo crossing the highway. Not your everyday experience. He identified the buffalo as that of our ABC Insurance Company's insured, Mark Abbey. The impact from the buffalo had severely damaged Mr. Plaintiff's truck.

After the petition was filed and Mr. Abbey questioned, he denied that the buffalo in question belonged to him. We asked how he knew that this was not his buffalo. He explained. His home was located near the site of the accident, but he kept his buffalo on a piece of land he rented that was about twenty-five miles away. The plaintiff insisted that the buffalo in question strayed to the crash site, and it had to be one of Mr. Abbey's, as no one else in the area had buffalo.

My Assignment: I was to locate the buffalo, or any buffalo, and take photos that would be shown to the plaintiff for ID purposes either before or at trial. I called Mr. Abbey, explaining what I needed, and asked if I could meet with him. He was not reluctant, just disgusted. He said he didn't know how he could help, but he agreed to a meeting. His place is way out in the country, and upon arrival, I expected to see at least one buffalo and certainly some cows and horses and other farm-type animals, but I didn't see any. I had arrived before the allotted time, so I roamed about the area on my own. I saw some animal pens, but no animals.

He arrived in his red 1959 Ford pickup truck, dressed in coveralls and cowboy boots, pretty much what you would expect. I asked him where all the animals were, and he said he'd have to drive me to where he housed them all. I said, "Let's go. I'll follow you!"

"I don't think so," he said. "You'd better go with me because your car will never make it through the pasture."

"Okay," I said and climbed into the passenger side of his truck. The first thing I noticed was no AC. The second thing I noticed was a beat-up Coke can on the dash and wondered why he would have an old beat-up

Coke can on the dash. Country fellow, strange habits, I thought. I soon found out. He was a tobacco chewer, and every so often, he'd spit out a stream of brown tobacco juice into the can as my stomach lurched.

Between performances of the above activity, we had an interesting conversation. It seems that Mr. Abbey owns many animals that he "rents out." He explained that buffalo are the best herders of all animals. Most laypeople think dogs are the best. Not so—buffalo. He rents most of his animals to movie studios and rodeos. He'd recently brought a mixture of animals to a circus in Tennessee.

We drove about forty-five minutes across the parish to a large pasture of land and spun up the road, through a gate, and bumped along the grasses as we approached the property he rented to house his brood. I spotted a giraffe, some sheep, a few cattle, hogs, horses, goats, and several buffalo. I noticed that the animals all had tags on their ears. I asked about that, and he told me that owners of animals generally tag their critters for identification purposes. I forget how he said it had occurred, but he mentioned that he had one buffalo that had died about a year prior, way before the accident in question. I told him how unfortunate that was, in that I was needing photos of the fellow. He said he still had the head, as he was going to have it stuffed and mounted. I questioned him about why it was still not done given it had been a year since the old boy passed. He explained that his taxidermist had been in the process of a big wedding and finally had recently had the nuptials and was currently honeymooning. He was supposed to work on the head when he returned. In the meantime, the head was in the freezer.

I needed to take some photographs. Mr. Abbey told me to wait in the truck. He said he would signal when I could get out so the animals wouldn't charge me. I was more than content to remain in the truck cab. He got a bag of feed from the truck bed and walked about 100 feet toward the animals. He made an animal sound, and they came to him as he tossed the feed onto the ground. As they began to eat, he signaled that I could get out. I did so and got some good long shots as well as close-ups. Don't think I'd have been so brave without Mr. Abbey's help.

"Can we go back to your house and get your buffalo head out of your freezer so I can take pictures?"

"Not quite that simple," he explained. He did not have enough room in his freezer, so he was storing it in the walk-in freezer of Gautreaux Meats in a nearby town. Mr. Gautreaux let him keep the head there until the taxidermy lovebirds got back from their cruise. "Is it just sitting in the freezer?" I asked.

"No, it's in a bucket in a plastic bag."

"Okay."

Later I called Mr. Gautreaux and explained, several times, who I was and what I needed. He ultimately agreed that I could come by his place and take the photos. When I got there, he was busy with customers, but I told him I didn't mind waiting until he was free. When he did free up, he brought me into his walk-in freezer and pulled a tin bucket from behind some cow carcasses hanging around. And there it was, looking up at me from inside the bucket and plastic bag. I asked Mr. Gautreaux if he could take it out for better photography purposes. He made several attempts to do so, but it appeared the head was stuck tight. I took the photos anyway. I did quite a bit of checking around, and no one knew of any other buffalo having ever been in the area.

At the time of trial, the plaintiff was shown the photos of the bucket head buffalo, and he immediately claimed that was the one! The very buffalo that he hit with his truck. Ashley asked, "Are you sure that is the buffalo in question?"

"Yes, oh, yes, that's the one!" he smiled.

Ashley said, "No further questions." I was next on the stand, and when questioned by Ashley, I assured the jury that after a thorough search of the area, there were no buffalo except the one in the bucket.

Mr. Gautreaux was next on the stand. Ashley, showing him the photo: "Is this the buffalo you have in your store freezer?"

"Yes, it is," he responded. Ashley: "How long have you had this buffalo in your freezer?"

"Over a year."

Ashley looked at the jury. "You will recall that the date of the accident in question was 5/13/2001. Mr. Gautreaux, would you have had that buffalo head in your freezer before that date?"

"Yes ma'am, way before that."

It was speculated that the plaintiff knew of Mr. Abbey's livelihood but was skimpy on the details. He knew the crash was near the Abbey property, he needed money, and the rest is history.

Case closed.

Bad Apple in this Bunch

Large insurance companies are very cautious in selecting their agents. They have to pass all sorts of tests and have to adhere to the strongest of rules. And they certainly must have upstanding morals. Scrutiny is at its strongest. We received a call from our big New Orleans law firm explaining that we are to meet in a small town in Ascension Parish that will remain nameless. This town had only one agent for this insurance company. We were to meet at the agent's office. We were to tell no one where we were going.

So, very curious, we met at the appointed place and time. Arthur Colbert and Timothy Ponce, two of the partners in the law firm, were already there as well as Frank Jones, one of the claims special investigators. Behind closed doors, Mr. Colbert explained our situation. The agent, John Doe, had been successful here for many years. He was highly respected in this small community. He had a wife and two small children, and they resided in a lovely home here. Mr. Doe was involved in many local charities and participated in much of the local school and church activities. He was also the director of the church choir.

Much to the surprise of all in the room, he had been accused by a local 15-year-old girl of courting her affections, promising love in return, and then breaking her heart. As a result, young Jane Smith had allegedly taken ill and had been hospitalized for emotional and mental problems. Mr. Doe was a handsome thirtysomething, very clean-cut, and presented himself to the community as a fine gentleman, excellent father, and husband. Most everyone had a high regard for him.

Mrs. Smith, Jane's mother, had approached Mr. Doe with her accusations and had threatened to expose him to the community and file a lawsuit for damages to her daughter and herself. Mr. Doe then contacted the higher-ups in the insurance company, which resulted in our meeting of this date. Expecting him to defend himself, we were all stunned when he admitted that he had tallied with the young girl's affections.

As choir director, he said he'd had reason to be in the company of the young girl at weekly choir practices and again on Sundays when they had church services. He had been the choir director for about two years and had experienced "crushes" from several young girls, which of course, he had ignored as appropriate. Young Jane was "very mature for her age," he explained.

He admitted she was beautiful in body and face and said she was "different" than the other female choir members. He recounted that for several months she began confiding in Mr. Doe, and they would have "talks" after choir practice and church. She told him about how she and her boyfriend had broken up and how upset and brokenhearted she was about it. He said that she would cry and "throw herself" into his arms, and he had tried to comfort her.

"Had you been intimate with her?" asked Mr. Colbert.

"No, I would not have done that," said Mr. Doe.

"Well, is anything she has accused you of true?" asked Mr. Colbert.

Mr. Doe went on to explain. "No, I was not intimate with her, but she began to come on to me, telling me she was in love with me. She would hug me and try to kiss me. Then she began to ask if I was happily married, and I told her that I was very happily married."

Mr. Colbert explained that Jane's mother has reported that Jane said Mr. Doe had promised to leave his wife, and that they would be married and live happily ever after. Mr. Doe clarified that he had not told her he would leave his wife, but he had to admit there was a great attraction to the girl. He acknowledged that they had kissed on several occasions, but it had never gone beyond that. He said that Jane began to get very "pushy" and kept begging him to leave his wife, insisting that she was much in love with him, and she would make him very happy.

Mr. Colbert, Mr. Ponce, and Mr. Jones thoroughly admonished Mr. Doe, and he, of course, was totally embarrassed and properly ashamed. It was very likely that they would relieve Mr. Doe of his agent duties, but at this point, they needed our help to save the reputation of this highly respected insurance company.

Our Assignment: We were to conduct surveillance on young Jane Smith and complete background checks on her as well as her mother. We were to attempt to determine if there was any way out of this mess and get any information that we could to assist in preventing Mrs. Smith from filing a lawsuit or going public.

It's challenging to complete background checks on minors, as they have little history. Plus, we have always had a problem with conducting surveillance on minors or investigating them. It makes you feel sort of perverted. But we went forth. We found out several things of assistance. One was that Jane did not appear to be upset or traumatized over the fact that Mr. Doe had broken things off. We also determined that she had a new boyfriend who would come to her house after school on most afternoons. She did not seem to have any problems at school. And, of most interest, we learned that her mother was seriously dating a black male. Jane and Ms. Smith were white females. We learned that Jane was very unhappy about the relationship, expressing so to her friends and teachers.

After developing this information, we got in touch with Mr. Colbert and asked if he'd gotten copies of the medical records from the hospital where Jane had been confined after her "breakdown." He assured us that he had those records. We told him about Jane being so unhappy with the relationship her mother was having with her boyfriend and asked if there was anything in the evaluation of her mental condition concerning that. He suggested we meet with him, and we'd go over the records together. We did so and found no mention of Jane being upset with her mother, but we also noted that there was no actual reference in the entire chart about John Doe, the choir director, or any mention of her broken heart. I pointed that out to Mr. Colbert.

In my early career, I spent a lot of time reviewing copies of medical records. Frequently, depending upon the hospital, I was permitted to pull the chart myself and go over the entire file and pull out what was needed to process the claim. Often there would be nurses' notes in the charts, added as afterthoughts. I suggested to Mr. Colbert that he request copies of the entire record, including nurses' notes and any handwritten notations made by the doctors.

Several days later, we got a call from him saying he had requested the entire record. Lo and behold, in the margins and at the end of some of the daily logs, there were three relevant comments by the nurses. The first said, "Jane expresses anger at her mother because she is dating a black man." Another, "Her mom came by today, and Jane asked her, 'Are you still seeing that man?' and asked her to leave." And finally, "Patient had been crying and said she was upset with her mother."

Case closed.

Mississippi Mutt

As you can imagine, animals can be a problem in any profession when you knock on the doors of strangers. In the early Wilson & Wilson days, Don and I drove over to rural Mississippi to work a case that required speaking to neighbors regarding a particular subject and his activities.

I have always been an animal lover, particularly dogs. When they know you have no fear and they can "smell" that you are not a threat and love them, which I do, they don't give you a problem. I had never had a problem with a dog in all these twenty-five or so years up to this point. Well, there was a time before this that I had approached a home that had an adult Doberman chained to the garage door. When I got out of my car, he bared his teeth, and I did my usual, "Hi, boy! Come on, come see me." He did, pulling the chain as far as it would go, pulling him upright and taller than me. He growled big time and had foam coming from his bared teeth! I must say that I was really glad he was chained. My feelings were hurt, though. This was my first experience with a dog with whom I couldn't make friends.

I've had some dog owners amazed that their dog, usually distrusting of strangers, would come to me.

Once I was working in Metairie, just outside of New Orleans. I had to interview a gentleman who had a car theft claim. He was working on a BBQ pit in his garage as I approached and identified myself. Soon his wife came out with a pit bull following behind. Now, we all know the reputation of pit bulls. This one was almost white and looked albino-ish, pink eyes and all. As soon as the dog spotted me, she walked up and started sniffing my leg and drooling all over my pants. "Now, Princess!" the owner said, "Don't bother the lady!" All the while, neither of them made any attempts to remove the menacing-looking dog. Princess kept rubbing, sniffing, and drooling, so I finally bent over and gave a couple of head pats, much to the delight of the dog. Mr. Insured looked at the dog and then at me, appearing stunned at both of us, and told his wife to take Princess back inside.

I digress. While in rural Mississippi, we had stopped at a few homes way out in the country. Don had always been cautious about strange dogs and fussed continuously at me for going up to them. On this occasion, as I walked to the steps leading up to the porch of a mobile home, I heard a growl come from underneath the trailer. I stepped back and saw a mixed-breed mutt with bared teeth. I was relaxed. I know that to make a friend with an unfriendly dog, one should get down to their level. So, I did my usual face-to-face with this dog, and he ran out from under and bit my foot right through my shoe! I couldn't believe it! My first dog bite! I'd broken my good record.

The homeowner came running out and told me that her dog hates strangers and invited us to go into the house right away. She told me that her grown son, who doesn't live at home anymore, came to see her the other day and the dog bit him too! Of course, she was afraid I was going to sue her, which I certainly would not do. We inspected my injury, and I assured her I would be fine and, of course, asked if the dog was current with his shots. She said he was.

Back in Baton Rouge, I went to my vet. You can tell I didn't know much about dog bites since I went to my vet instead of my doctor. He said to me that even if the dog owner states the dog has had its shots, I should get mine anyway. He said he could give it to me, but if anyone found out about it, he would lose his license. I didn't know that, either. He also instructed me to get a tetanus shot and penicillin as well. So, I did.

My doctor asked me when I was going to give up this hazardous profession. I told him, "Never!"

Ragin' Cajun

After my experience with the Mississippi Mutt, I was much more cautious when approaching strange dogs. But I continued to make friends with every one of them, and after several years I forgot about it and relaxed back into my old habits.

I had another case in Cajun country. Mr. Baxter had backed his car out of his driveway in Mamou, Louisiana, and hit a vehicle passing down his street, bringing a suit against him. I was to complete a scene investigation and take photos where the accident took place. I had called ahead to make an appointment with him.

When I got to his house, I parked on the street, and as I walked onto his driveway, I noted a beautiful adult red-coated dog. He was a husky-chow mix. I approached him in my usual manner, getting low to his level, when he popped up, growled, bared his teeth. I backed up but not fast enough, and he charged and bit me right on the thigh, tearing through my pants. He was tethered. About that time, Mr. Baxter came running out of the house, extremely upset. He ushered me into his home and offered the use of his bathroom along with antiseptic and bandages.

In checking, I found I did have a pretty bad injury. The tear was in the shape of the dog's teeth. I washed it out, bandaged it up, and went on about my business, taking the photos and getting the details from Mr. Baxter. During my entire stay, he must have apologized a dozen times. I told him from the beginning that it was entirely my fault. I should not have approached the dog, and he had him properly chained. As I was leaving, he insisted that I send him any medical bills and did assure me that the dog was current in his shots.

This time I went first to my doctor and second to my vet, who told me that a husky-chow mix will ensure a vicious animal and that I should have known better. I never get any sympathy!

My doctor again wanted to know when I was going to quit this foolishness and gave me my shots and a prescription for antibiotics. By this time, I was earning my name of Granny P.I., and I was on Medicare, so I just sent Mr. Baxter a bill for the antibiotics, after which he promptly mailed me a check with still another apology.

I wonder how long it was following this incident before he finally relaxed and realized that I was not going to sue.

I still have a scar.

Contacts

You can imagine that I get many cases that involve people on financial assistance. Much of the time, these folks are looking for as much free money as they can get. I always say, if they'd spend as much time and effort trying to find a job as they do trying to buck the system, they'd be multi-millionaires. This case involved a woman who'd had an alleged "slip and fall" at a grocery store in Lake Charles. At the time of the incident, she was with her good friend, Carlota Jackson of Lake Charles. The claimant was Viola Smith. My job was to locate Carlota and obtained a recorded statement from her as to her memory of what took place at the time of the incident.

I generally verify the address before I proceed, which saves time, however, in this case, the address was on my way, so I stopped by the house first. No one was home, and it was apparent that no one lived there. But there was mail in the box, addressed to Carlota Jackson. So, off I went to check my sources. All information pointed to the fact that Ms. Jackson resided there. She did have several addresses prior to that one, but none since. I learned that Carlota was on welfare, food stamps, Social

Security disability, and every other kind of government-supported assistance. She had several children and no husband. She also had several misdemeanors on file. I came back to Baton Rouge stumped, but not defeated.

People ask me all the time, "You must have a lot of contacts," in that I'm 97 percent successful in locating people. That is not the case for the most part. You know the old name "gumshoe" for a P.I.? Well, it is a good description. I do most of my work on the street. I have had contacts in the past, and they are great. But contacts don't hang around. They get fired, die, and sometimes just don't want to help anymore.

There was an old friend of my husband's who ran credit checks for a while, but he got fired. There was another old friend who did the same until her husband found out about it and told her not to do it anymore. He did some P.I. work on the side, so I think that was the real reason why. There was a state trooper who used to run out-of-state license plates for me. I think she was found out because the last time I called her, she declined. I understand. Their jobs can be in jeopardy. There was a fellow who worked for the state risk insurance department. He died. There was a firefighter who helped me for a while, but he wanted a little more personal attention than I was willing to give! My husband's cousin's brother worked for the telephone company, and he got unlisted telephone numbers for us, but he retired. You get the picture.

In the case of Carlota Jackson, I had a good friend who worked for the state. I won't go into any more than that, but she was able to help. I would never ask her unless I had tried everything else. She checked for me but came up with the same old address I had, which was good as of a week ago. We were puzzled. We decided that someone must be picking up her checks for her at that address. She did find out, however, that her fifteen-year-old daughter, who was also on government assistance, recently updated her address along with her newborn baby daughter. Her current address was in Lake Charles, Louisiana. Jackpot! We had a pretty good idea that was where the new grandma was living.

Within the next day or so, back to Lake Charles I went. The address was located in government-assisted housing in a not-so-lovely part of town. This was before GPS, so I stopped at one of the best places to get directions, the fire station on one of the main roads through town. Several firefighters showed me on their city map how to get there. They looked at Granny P.I. and suggested that I might consider bringing some strong bodyguard type with me due to the neighborhood. I told them I appreciated the heads up, but that I'd be fine. This was not my first time.

When I got there, I drove around to get a feel for the place. I parked the shortest distance from the rear entrance that I could find and walked over to the door to 15 and knocked several times. Finally, a female voice from the other side asked who it was. I shouted, "Nancy Wilson, representing ABC Insurance about your being a witness to Viola Smith's fall at the store!" She thought about that for a minute or two and opened the door.

Carlota was there, carrying a baby about one week old, and on the sofa was the fifteen-year-old mother. I went in and continued to explain why I was there. Carlota said she would give a statement, but she wanted Ms. Smith to be present—was that okay? We do not get statements from witnesses with the claimant present nor in the presence of any other witnesses, but one must use one's common sense, and, in these circumstances, I knew that was the only way I would get this accomplished. She pulled out her cell phone and called the claimant.

She got there about thirty minutes later. As they say in the trade, she entered the residence showing no signs of disability, not wearing a brace, or using a cane or any other walking aid. I began taking the recorded statement and, not surprisingly, Ms. Claimant stopped to interject corrections several times during the recording. This was advantageous, however, since the claimant was also heard on the tape, proving that the witness was being coached. She'd say, "No, Carlota, that's not how it happened, it was so and so? Remember?"

"Oh, yeah, that's right," Carlota would say, and so on.

As I was leaving and thanking all parties involved, Carlota finally had a rude awakening! "Hey, how in the hell did you find me, anyway?" And she was not a happy camper.

I explained, "It wasn't easy. I'll tell you that!!" And I had that door opened and scooted my little old self out and over to my car, keys in hand, jumped in my car as fast as I could as I watched both ladies, each twice my size, running around the corner as I headed out of the parking lot.

Of course, as the witness and the disabled claimant came charging through the parking lot, I just happened to have my camera up and running over my shoulder.

Lesbians and Pervert Attorneys

I was referred to this new attorney by one of my old clients. I suspect he was somewhat shocked when I entered his office. By this time, I was befitting the Granny P.I. name given to me by some clients. I think I was about sixty-two when I first met Kent Carrington. Kent was in his late thirties at this time, must have weighed at least 300 pounds. He was a real charmer.

We sat down in his office. By we, I mean myself, Kent, and his partner, mild-mannered young Harry. Harry's personality was directly opposite of Kent's. Kent began to go over the case with me. Our client was a large trucking firm that covers the entire U.S. There had been an accident between one of our trucks and the passenger plaintiff. The plaintiff is from Delcambre, Louisiana, and the accident occurred on I-10 in Cajun country. Our primary witness was in the passenger seat at the time of the accident, and there were two lesbian passengers in the backseat. One of those gay ladies was the plaintiff, who was claiming injuries.

It was apparent after about five minutes that Kent was trying to determine if this little old lady P.I. could handle a job involving lesbians. He intentionally used every four-letter word in the book in describing the accident, our witness, and especially the activities that our witness observed in the backseat of the car just before the accident. I learned during this case that Kent could get overly zealous as he gets further involved in a case. I also determined that he did some pretty reckless and sometimes stupid things.

My Assignment: I was to locate Brenda LeBlanc, our primary witness. I was to become her best friend and cultivate her to be on our side and have her divulge as much dirt on the plaintiff that we could. Sometimes that works, and sometimes it doesn't. My experience in this business is that Kent was spending way too much money in this regard. But, what the heck, he's the boss and writes the check, so I do whatever he wants.

I did locate young Brenda LeBlanc, who was living in small-town Cajun, Louisiana, in a mobile home. She was in a shaky marriage, and she also had a very unstable background. She was into drugs and had a record involving bad checks and financial difficulties. When I first spoke to her, she was quiet and shy. She did remember the accident and had a pretty good recollection of the goings-on in the backseat of the car. We talked for a good while, and she began to tell me about her marital problems. She also had issues with her family, and they were pretty much estranged. After I spoke with her, I called Kent, who was thrilled with the information I had so far. He wanted to set up a meeting with Brenda to take her deposition. We agreed that he, Harry, a court reporter, and I would meet with her at her favorite little cafe in Delcambre a few days later.

So, there we were, the four of us driving down to Delcambre at Bertrand's Cafe, arriving at 10 a.m. We took up a booth and waited for our star witness. It began to look like she was a no-show when she finally appeared at 10:25 a.m. You could tell she was intimidated by Kent. We all tried to relax her, and finally, she settled down and agreed to be recorded. To this date, I think Kent just gets off by getting into sexual things. I found out as I worked with him that he had an addiction to coke and prostitutes.

As we got into the statement, he got overly excited as Brenda began explaining the activities in the backseat. I won't go into the details here, but you get the picture. He next wanted to know how long she had known the backseat couple. He asked her if she'd been with them at any social functions, having to explain to her what social functions meant. She told him she'd been at a bar with them one time. He wanted to know in detail. She described how they "close danced" in the bar and kissed. Kent loved this. What else did they do?

"Well, they went outside for a while," she reported.

"What did they do outside?" Kent asked.

"Well, you know, they ... " she hesitated.

Kent asked, "Oh, well, come on now. What did they do?"

"Oh, they did the nasty," Brenda shyly said.

Kent was thrilled!

I was sitting there thinking, this law firm is paying for this! What the heck does this have to do with anything!

As the case progressed and it was getting closer to the trial date, Kent wanted me to go down to Delcambre to make sure our star was still being cooperative and that she understood that the trial date was up and coming. So, off I went. When I got to Brenda's trailer, there was no one there. I did some checking about and found out that she was in jail on multiple worthless check charges. I called Kent, and we agreed that I would talk to her.

I went to the Vermilion Parish jail and went through the process of going through the scanner, checking my purse and briefcase, and being tagged and allowed to enter. I was placed in a small office, as they did not have any other private place where we could talk. In a short while, Brenda came in and just burst into tears. I gave her a big hug, and she held on for dear life. Her husband and her parents and siblings were doing nothing to help her. She didn't know when she would ever get out of jail. She could not bond herself out, as she had no money. She begged for me to help her. I gave her a few dollars for cigarettes and told her I'd talk to Kent and see what we could do.

I left and called Kent, who decided he would put up her bond, get her out of jail, and get her cleaned up and ready to testify. And he did. I was not required to go to the trial. That was fine with me. I think I would have been embarrassed to have been a part of this testimony.

We lost the case.

He Wore His Best Orange Coveralls

This occurred about thirty or so years ago. The case involved a plaintiff who'd had a "slip and fall" in her home. Her husband was her only witness, as he had been in the house when she fell and called 911. They are now divorced, and he is in jail in Washington Parish in east Louisiana. My job was to go to the jail and obtain a recorded statement from him as to the events surrounding his wife's accident. I accepted the job, phoned the jail, and made an appointment to interview the jailbird at 10 a.m. the following date. The local sheriff was pleasant and cooperative. I arrived early in Washington Parish, where I did some background searching on Mr. Walker Landry, as I sure wanted to know why he was in the pokey. It turned out that he was in jail for molesting his ten-year-old stepdaughter. No wonder why his wife divorced him!

I arrived at the jail right on time, and the sheriff and his deputy were like Andy and Barney. The big city lady P.I. was a guest at their facility, and they were going to accommodate. They had been waiting for me, and the sheriff escorted me up the stairs where the jail was, above the office. They offered me their best chair and insisted on serving coffee. I didn't tell them that I don't drink coffee, as I didn't want to hurt their feelings.

After our little visit, I told them I needed to get on with the interview. Sheriff Taylor apologized for their facility and told me the only place they could arrange a meeting was in the "Library." I told him that it would be perfectly acceptable. He escorted me into a room that turned out to be not much bigger than a closet. There was a small desk and a straight-back chair, and the shelves only contained about ten books! Sheriff Taylor brought a second chair for me. Mr. Landry was seated in the straight-back chair in his neatly pressed orange jumpsuit. He was cuffed, clean-shaven, and his hair was neatly combed. He was very pale—from lack of sun, I guessed.

I got my recorded statement from him. He was very much the gentleman. I would never have guessed that he was a child molester. After we were through, Andy and Barney told me what a pleasure it had been to meet me and to come back again whenever I was in the neighborhood. Since then, I have contacted Sheriff Taylor several times, and he has been most helpful if I have a problem in Washington Parish. And he never failed to tell me how much they had enjoyed my visit.

Murder One

Getting recorded statements is not my favorite thing. Most people get statement fright when they see the Recorder. In this case, we had an insured who lived in small-town Bayou Goula, Louisiana; however, he was in jail in the East Baton Rouge Parish Prison in Baton Rouge. It seems he had killed his ex-girlfriend. This case resulted from the fact that he was at the gas station in Bayou Goula when the claimant alleged that our insured hit him in the parking lot when he was walking across it. This was, of course, before he was arrested in the murder charge.

My Assignment: I was to get a recorded statement from him as to what occurred at the gas station. I called ahead to get instructions. East Baton Rouge Parish Prison is located out by the airport in north Baton Rouge. One of the complaints the locals have about that is when out-of-towners come to visit, the first thing they see is the jail. On the day of my meeting with Murder One, I parked in the lot labeled "Visitors" and went over to the guard in the gatehouse. She was an intimidating 300-pound black female. "What do you want?" she bellowed. I explained my purpose, and

122

she instructed me to "Move your vehicle!" indicating a parking area nearby. I moved my vehicle and returned to her guardhouse, where she stripped me of everything except my briefcase and recorder, which were tagged.

I entered the jail through the main entrance and approached the officer at Information. I explained my purpose once again, and he told me to have a seat. I did. About five minutes later, another guard came through a different entrance and signaled me forward. We walked to Gate One, which was barred and double-locked. He unlocked, and we passed, walking to Gate Two, which was in similar condition as Gate One. He unlocked, and we walked to Gate Three, which was identical. We then entered the actual jail, at which point we approached the dispatcher enclosed in a small, bulletproof office housing two guards, a switchboard, phones, computers, and weapons. To the left of this structure stood an orange-clad black male. There were no cuffs, no chains, and zero restraints.

The second guard introduced me to the third guard, who said, "Here he is," pointing to the orange gentleman. The second guard escorted Murder One and my little old self to a small room containing a small table and two chairs. We sat, and Guard Two left, closed the door, and locked it! Now I'm locked in with him, and there's no security camera in sight. I was dumbfounded! I had been in this jail several years before, and I interviewed my convict in the cafeteria with a security guard seated nearby. Of course, that inmate was only a thief or something. This one was in for the big one. Oh well, I told myself, we had heard years ago from a higher-up in the state police that the safest prisoners are Murder Ones because they generally act in a one-time insane rage and don't do it again. So, I went forth.

I explained who I was, who I was representing, and that I needed a recorded statement from him as to his recollection of the incident in question. He was very well-behaved and had a good recollection of the incident. He told me that the claimant in this case was the Town Drunk and that he was always faking accidents and making claims. Everyone in town knew about him. So, I got my statement.

I wasn't sure how to proceed next, so I rose and knocked on the door from within, and Guard Two came and got us. Murder One simply got up and walked to our left down the hall, alone, no escort. Guard Two escorted me through all the gates again. On our way out, I commented, "Your inmate seems to be a pretty nice guy." He said, "They all are. It's the circle. They are raised by single mothers who were raised by single mothers. The males all grow up and see how many young girls they can get pregnant. It's a status thing. They brag about it to one another. They have no fathers. They don't go to church. They have no morals and don't even know what morals are. And they end up in here."

Shortly after my interview with Mr. One, I drove over to Iberville Parish and did a background on the claimant. I found out that our witness was right. He is known as the Town Drunk in Bayou Goula and surrounding areas. He also has a history of filing personal injury lawsuits.

Four Men and a Car

This case occurred in my very early days. This was before getting recorded statements and, instead, getting written ones signed by the subject. This subject was on disability, and we had our yearly investigation to determine what his current activities were, if he was able to return to work, and how his health was. Johnsville is a tiny place on the west side of the Mississippi River. As I recall, there are a total of three streets that stretch from the river to the highway. The main street is Cemetery Lane. As small as the town is, there is a lot of crime.

I was driving Don's brand-new Pontiac on this occasion and drove down Cemetery Lane on an overcast day. It had been raining all night, and I got there at 9:30 a.m. All the streets in Johnsville are narrow, having ditches on either side of the street rather than sidewalks. I drove down the street to River Road and turned around, came back, and parked in front of Mr. Bartlett's house. I parked as much off the road as I could to let other vehicles pass by. I then went through the gate, down the walkway, and knocked on the door. Mrs. Bartlett answered the door and graciously allowed me to enter the residence. I took my statement from the wheelchaired Mr. Bartlett, bid them farewell, and exited the home.

As I walked toward the street, I looked up and saw that my car had slid off the road into the ditch. There was no way I would be able to get the vehicle up out of the ditch and down the road. As I was pondering my situation, I observed four of the biggest guys I'd ever seen sauntering up the road toward me and my car! As they got closer, they began to slow their pace. I figured I was either going to be done in or saved. "Good morning!" I said. "You can see that I have quite a problem. Would you gentlemen help me to get my car out of this ditch?"

The Leader Large responded, "We don't do stuff for free."

All I had with me was a five-dollar bill that was supposed to be for my lunch. I said, "All I have is $5."

They looked from one to the other. I held my breath. Would they hit me over the head for five bucks? Maybe not. Maybe they'd feel sorry for me and try to push the car out of the ditch. No, they did neither. Instead, two of them stood at the front of the car, and two stood at the rear. All at one time, they picked the car up out of the ditch and set it down in the street. They didn't even need a second try!

With my mouth hanging open, I got the five-dollar bill out of my purse. I gave it to Mr. Large, apologized for not having more, thanked them, got into the new muddy Pontiac, and drove off down Cemetery Lane, counting my blessings that I got out clean without a headstone with RIP Nancy Jane on it!

Body Odor, Smoke Smells & Lice

Occasionally I need to pick up and bring subjects or witnesses to trial or to depositions or simply to meet with our attorney because they don't have any other way to get there. In this case, our attorney was my favorite charmer and fat guy, Bob Burton. Our star witness was Audra Stark from a tiny rural town by the name of Holden, Louisiana. I had located her living with one of the other witnesses, Ron Frederick, and they lived in a box of a trailer about fourteen-feet-by-ten-feet on a dirt road off Highway 43. I was to bring Ron in with us as well.

The first time I picked them up, I had a good taste of what I had in store, knowing that I would be bringing them in several more times. Audra climbed in the front seat with me, Ron in the backseat with their buddy, Billy Ray Parker. All were smokers. I don't allow smoking in my car. However, we needed these folks to be cooperative. They didn't ask if it was okay to smoke. I also noticed a nasty body odor. From the looks of their "home," it is highly possible they did not have a shower. So, I rolled down my window and managed. As we approached Baton Rouge and Bob's offices, Audra proceeded to tell me, "Oh, no, when Bob picked us up, he turned here and went down Jefferson Highway!"

"Oh," I said, "Bob has picked you up before?"

"Oh, yeah, the first time we were here, he brought us."

Now I knew why it was now my job to pick this group up! After we got there, I rolled all my windows down in hopes that I could air out my car, or maybe it would be stolen, and I could get another one!

As soon as I got Bob alone, I said, "Bob, they all smell, and they all smoke, and my car smells awful!!" He said, "We'll pay to have your car cleaned when this is all over." Of course, in the meantime, I got to live with the odor. But that's why I get paid these big bucks, I told myself. On the way back, Audra ran out of cigarettes, both boys needed a beer, and they all decided they needed to stop at McDonald's. No one had any money and, besides, Bob paid for lunch last time. Good old Bob.

I was fortunate in that I got to pick them up several more times. The last time was five days before the trial. I asked, "You mean I get to pick them up again for trial?"

"No, no," I was told, "we have to get Audra cleaned up before trial, and it will take several days."

It seems that when they had taken her to the hairdresser for a shampoo, they found she had lice!

Now I was to check them all into a motel, one room for Audra and one for Ron and Billy Ray. Then I was to buy a de-licing kit at Walgreens and give Audra two treatments a day, lastly on trial day, and then bring her back to Hair Station for a cut, dry, and style. It seems the hairdresser would not allow her back until she was de-liced. I was also to get her a new outfit from head to toe and hopefully burn the clothes she was wearing and, for God's sake, have her take a bath. I couldn't wait to take on the de-licing duties! And her teeth! There were several missing, and I don't think she knew how to brush and "What's flossing?" she wanted to know.

I checked them into the Marriott. As much as I didn't want to, I got smoking rooms. I was afraid they wouldn't adhere to the rules and smoke anyway. I didn't want another headache. I told the fellows to take care of themselves as I got Audra to bathe and, for now, get into some clean clothes. She was pretty good about doing as asked. We went to Stein-Mart and got shoes, underwear, a smart pantsuit, and some conservative jewelry. I did my de-licing, gave them dinner and cigarette money, and took off in my smelly car. I did the daily hair thing for the rest of the week, and we went to the hairdresser on the morning of the trial. I must say, even with the teeth problem, she looked lovely. Ron had brought his "best clothes." At least they were clean. I brought them all to the office, and Bob was delighted. He suggested that Audra keep her mouth closed except to testify, and off we all went to the courthouse.

After all this, we lost the case. Our plaintiff had been electrocuted by climbing on an electrical structure owned by the local electric company. He'd climbed over the fence, onto the tower, and slipped and was severely burned, resulting in bad scarring and being in a wheelchair for the rest of his life. We contended that they should have had better prevention in place to keep people out. Our witnesses had been present at the time of the accident. It seems the electric company had their witness, who testified that our plaintiff had been drinking beer and smoking weed before he decided to climb onto the electrical unit.

Case closed.

New Orleans Ladies

This case came about a claim resulting in alleged foundation damage to the residence insured by ABC Insurance Company. The homeowner was alleging that an explosion at a nearby plant had caused the damage.

My Assignment: I was to meet the insured and get a statement as to what had happened. I knew the address was in the Desire Projects, which is mostly government housing, and one of the least desirable areas in New Orleans, despite the name. As long as I have an appointment, I generally feel relatively safe and comfortable going to these areas. I called Ms. Insured, and we made an appointment for 10 a.m. on a Monday.

I pulled up to the house, which was a smallish blond brick with typical New Orleans bric-a-brac decor around the front porch. I was a little taken aback when she opened the door. She was a reasonably attractive lady in her late forties. She was perfectly made up, a little heavily so. She had her hair curled and swept up on her head with a curl dangling down in front of each ear and down the back of her neck. She was wearing a beige nighty and peignoir set and dangling gold earrings and necklaces along with gold slippers. She had a ring on almost every finger and numerous gold bracelets.

She invited me in, and I was stunned to note the furniture and decor. I could see only the living room and dining area. All of the furniture was gold or white, covered with a clear plastic covering. The drapes and walls were all in bright red or pink. The tables were all gold and white, and the ashtrays and lamps were all white and gold. I didn't want to sit on the plastic, but I didn't have any choice. Again, when invited to sit, we cannot be rude or unpleasant. So sit, I did, on a far end of the sofa, and Ms. Insured sat in a lounge chair.

We began the recorded statement, during which she received several phone calls. Each time it rang, she checked her caller ID and excused herself, saying it was a business call. When I got to the part of the interview where I asked where she was employed, she explained that she "works for herself out of her home." She said that she does "counseling."

After the initial identifying questions, we got down to the nitty-gritty of the complaint. Ms. Insured said she had heard a loud noise that shook the house "like an earthquake" for several moments and then stopped. She knew immediately what it was because she'd experienced the same thing before. We always ask if there was anyone at the residence beside herself who witnessed the incident. She said, "Well, one of my clients was here at the time. Sometimes they spend the night." We asked for name and number, but she "couldn't remember who he was."

Afterward, I told my daughter and son-in-law, who was a police officer at the time, about this experience. He said, "Well, Ma, you know you had just interviewed a hooker." I told him I'd guessed as much. It turned out that Ms. Insured had experienced the same thing before, filed a claim, got an adjuster out there, and cashed her check but never got the foundation repaired. She thought she'd just try it again just in case.

SUBPOENAS

Nancy Wilson celebrating another successful case closed!

Serving the Mafia

Serving subpoenas is not my favorite of duties. If it's easy, it's boring. If it's hard, it's pretty much a pain in the rear. Sometimes, however, it can be gratifying.

My Assignment: I had to serve a trial subpoena to a young white male in his mid-twenties who was from the New Orleans/Jefferson Parish area. Generally, they will give the subpoenas to the sheriff's deputy, and he is to make a couple of attempts. If he is unable to serve, they do what is called a Due and Diligent service. They then have the judge appoint someone like me as a private process server. We private process servers generally try a lot harder than the sheriff deputies do. So, I got my assignment to serve Arturo Russo of New Orleans.

It was the same address given to the deputy to no avail, but I have to make an attempt there anyway. The address was a vacant lot. So, I checked with my "usual and confidentials." In doing so, I did not locate any address for Arturo, but I did determine that his father was Arturo Russo, Sr. In further checking, I found out that Art Sr. worked for a used car lot in Metairie. I drove over to that car lot and was able to speak with Art Sr.

Art Sr. was a short, heavyset, black-haired, typical Italian fellow in his late forties. Very personable, with typical used-car-salesman speak. Oh, he was more than pleased to talk to the young lady process server. But, so sorry to say, he and Art Jr. had had a falling out some time ago and, no, he had no idea where Junior was at this time. No, none at all. No, he had no idea who might know where he might be.

"So, I'm sorry I can't be of more help, young lady, but would you like to have a drink later on?"

"No, thanks," I replied.

But I certainly am not through yet, I said to myself. I knew old Art Sr. was full of bull, being married at this time to one of your savvier car salesmen myself! And now, he'd made me mad. Do not patronize me! I'm a lady private eye, and I have a job to do, and, by God, I'm going to do it!

In checking Art Sr. out with my "usual and confidentials," I found out that he was a member of the New Orleans Mafioso. I also found out that old Art Sr. had quite a bit of property in the Orleans/Jefferson Parish area and some in the outlying parishes as well. I spread my territory out into the River Parishes and ultimately learned that he had several residential properties. I checked each of them out and finally learned that he had purchased a property in LaPlace, Louisiana, in a nondescript subdivision, and that he had Junior holed up right there!

By now, I'd obtained a photo ID of Junior. I'd gone by the house several times and determined what he drove. Now, despite the brave female P.I. that I'd become, I still was not ready to approach a Mafioso son with an unwanted subpoena without some assistance. I have a very dear friend who is originally from the New Orleans area. At that time, he was about thirtyish. He is six-foot-six, weighs a good 250 pounds, and has one of the scariest looks about him that you have ever seen. He is also a licensed P.I., and I worked for him years ago. We love each other dearly and have always been willing to help each other out.

So, I called up Elliot and asked if he'd go with me as a bodyguard so I could serve this guy. He immediately agreed. We met at an agreed place and time, during the day, and went to LaPlace in my van. We drove to Junior's house, and no car was there. Well, I decided to try anyway, but no one came to the door. We agreed to try again another day.

About a week later, I was going from Baton Rouge back to New Orleans on another assignment when I decided to just swing by Junior's house. I'm in my dark blue Astro van, alone. As l drove up to his house, I saw Junior drive into the driveway, get out of his car, and go into the house. I said to myself, "Well, kiddo, what the heck. He's there. Give it a shot." I pulled in front of his house. I put the subpoena in my purse and left the van running. Doing my best impersonation of a lost female, I went to the carport door, knocked, and Junior opened the back door. I said, "Are you Arturo Russo?"

He said, "Yes."

I said, "I have this for you," and gave him the subpoena. He looked at it as I was turning toward my van, and he just said, "Oh, thank you!"

I think he was so stunned that he didn't know what else to say. I have always wondered what Papa Russo had to say about that!

Was it a Him? She? Or Shim?

I'll never forget the day I met with my favorite attorney on this one. He is Drew Grainger with his law firm in Baton Rouge. And I have him to thank for matching Wilson & Wilson with one of the largest insurance companies in the U.S. I very rarely get involved in domestic cases, but this was too good to pass up.

This husband, Simon Taylor, and his wife, Mary Ann Taylor, were already divorced, and Mary Ann got custody of the two very young children, a son and a daughter. About a year after the divorce, Mary Ann started seriously dating someone described as a "strange-looking and acting fellow." He was about six feet tall and 225 pounds, with a dark complexion and black hair. While he did not live with Mary Ann, he apparently spent a good deal of time at her house and had been seen by the neighbors going into her home when she was not there.

As weeks passed, Simon heard that this guy had started banging her around. Simon was becoming more and more concerned about the children and their safety. Simon had been keeping his sister updated on the situation, and one day she was visiting Mary Ann and the kids when she happened to get a peek into the boyfriend's wallet. The boyfriend had said his name was Leonard Borgia. As most states do, Louisiana driver's licenses have a photo ID with height and weight, which all matched Leonard, but the name on the license was Linda Borgia, not Leonard Borgia. In the sex slot, it had "F" and not "M"!

Simon's sister freaked. She didn't immediately say anything to Mary Ann, but as soon as she could discretely make her exit, she ran over to Simon's office with this information. Since my attorney David had handled the divorce, Simon came directly to him. Proceedings were initiated for a change of custody, which greatly upset Mary Ann, who was ultimately deposed.

When David called me in, it was after that deposition. David explained the whole case to me and went into the results of the testimony. It seems Mary Ann is quite a naive young lady as well as quiet and shy. David tried to be sympathetic and sensitive in the matter. He asked her what Leonard's gender was. Male. Were they intimate? Yes. Did they have penetration? Yes. Did Leonard have normal male genitals? Yes. Umm, what did they "feel like?" "Well, normal."

David: "What did they look like?"

Mary Ann: "Well, I've never seen them."

David, astonished: "You've had penetration, but you've never seen his genitals?"

Mary Ann: "No. It's always been in the dark."

David: "So in all these months that you've had intercourse, you've never seen his genitals?"

Mary Ann: "No."

David: "Didn't you find that strange?"

Mary Ann: "Well, yes, but it was okay with me."

David: "Has Leonard ever said anything about a sex change?"

Mary Ann: "No."

David: "Is Leonard a female or a male?"

Mary Ann: "He's a male."

In further questioning, David found out that Mary Ann did not know where Leonard lives, but she said it was somewhere in or around New Orleans. She didn't know if he'd ever been married before, nothing about his personal life. She did know that he is a house painter, that he calls himself "Leonardo," and that his business is "Da Vinci's Masterpieces."

My assignment: I was to locate Leonard and serve him with a deposition subpoena.

Leonard was not an easy person to find. In making my usual inquiries, I learned that his business was pretty active in the areas outside of New Orleans. I was able to locate several customers of Leonard's, and, in doing so, I did get a look at his business panel truck several times. I also learned that there had been several former girlfriends in this area as well. Apparently, everyone knows that Leonard is Linda Borgia, but he/she is so big and manly that everyone thinks of her like him. They also refer to him as Leonardo Da Vinci, and that's who he thinks he is. He is a frustrated artist and is thought of locally as a "weirdo." No kidding. He has a lot of emotional problems. Most people are afraid of him, and he has been violent in the past. I confirmed several arrests for crimes involving battery, assault, etc.

I finally did locate Linda/Leonard/Leonardo/Da Vinci/Borgia. He was living on the second floor with a female "friend." I had my subpoena. I parked my car under a shade tree on the boulevard across the street from the house. I knew that Leonard was expecting to be served and did not want to be deposed. The second floor was accessed by a white staircase on the left side of the house, accessible from the rear. After about a forty-five-minute wait, I saw him drive to the back of the house in the Da Vinci's Masterpieces truck and then enter the residence. Once he was inside, I got out of my car, climbed the stairs, and knocked on the door. His roomie answered my knock, and I asked to see Leonard. I could see him standing toward the rear of the room behind the roomie. He would not come forward. I said to him, "I have this for you" and showed him the subpoena.

He responded, "I'm not him."

I said, "Yes, you are," and tossed the subpoena into the room. I said, "We are face to face, and you have been served."

And that is the law. Once you have ID'd the subject, even if he refuses to accept, he, she, or shim is still served.

Kicked Out of Dodge

This was a case in which I was to serve a trial subpoena to an elderly gentleman.

Dave Pritchard lived in an impoverished area of our fair city of Baton Rouge. This area has been this way for as long as I can remember. It was also high in crime, prostitution, and drug traffic. I'm used to that, and it doesn't bother me. Well, not too much. I've learned how to handle myself in these situations. But this one turned out to be a little different!

The first thing I do, of course, is to locate the house. I had the municipal number 10354 Birdsong Street. In this particular neighborhood, more often than not, the houses do not have municipal numbers on them or their mailboxes, which are out on the street. So, I needed to drive around and try and figure out which house was 10354. I finally located it and approached the front door, getting no response. I left the area but came back the next day with the same results.

As I was leaving the subdivision, a sheriff's unit pulled up behind me, so I pulled over. The driver was in plain clothes. The deputy signaled at the window for me to roll it down. He asked me what I was doing.

I explained that I am a P.I. and that I have been appointed as a private processor to serve a subpoena. I showed it to him. He said, "I live in this subdivision, and I've gotten several calls from the residents in here complaining that you have been driving around." He went on to say, "You have no business being in here, and I'm telling you not to come back." I explained that I had to serve the subpoena, and he told me I would have to find another way to do that or get someone else to do the job. He would not understand the particulars of the situation, so I just agreed not to return and left, somewhat shaken.

Now what? So, I reached out to my "usual and confidentials." I was able to find a relative with a listed telephone number, and I contacted her under a pretext. I didn't think she would be helpful if told her I needed to serve her nephew with a trial subpoena. She revealed that old Dave was in the hospital, so I contacted a couple of the local hospitals and found out in which one Dave Pritchard was a patient. He was in room 1016. I'd never served anyone in the hospital before and wasn't exactly sure how to go about doing it. After thinking it over, I figured I just go there, walk in his room, and serve the subpoena. What's the problem with that?

So, that's what I did. I parked in the hospital parking lot. I walked through the entrance. I asked where room 1016 was and was told it was on the third floor. I took the elevator up. I walked down the corridor to the second to last room on the left. The door was open. Mr. Pritchard was lying in bed, hooked up to several tubes. Mrs. Pritchard was sitting in a chair by the bed reading a magazine. I walked in, Mrs. Pritchard looked up questioningly, and I said, "Is this Mr. Dave Pritchard?" She said, "Yes." I laid the subpoena on the bed and left.

Screw you, Deputy. Case closed.

Subpoena Vaccine

I may be the only person I know who doesn't mind getting a subpoena. There are a few who are expecting them—some professional people such as doctors, who consider it part of the territory. Almost everyone else avoids them like the plague. I think if there were a vaccine against subpoenas, some people would take it no matter the cost. I had one such person just the past year.

This fellow is a developer who builds big hotels, restaurants, office buildings, and shopping centers. I also serve petitions. For those who may not know, when someone is filing suit against a defendant, that defendant has to be served the complaint. If he or she is not served with that document, the case cannot go forward. In this particular case, I found out that many, I mean many, suits involving monies owed have been filed against this guy, and almost none, if any, had ever actually been served. I found this out after my first effort. This guy would die for a Petition Vaccine.

The address I had for service was his office. When I got there, I asked his staff if he was in. "No, he's not in today."

"When will he be back?" I asked.

They exchanged looks. "We don't know. He comes and goes."

"I can just leave this with one of you ladies, then," I say, holding up my plain brown envelope containing the petition.

"Mr. Jones has instructed us that we cannot accept packages for him under any circumstances."

"Oh, really? I've never run into a situation where someone in the office can't accept for their employer," I continue.

"Well, we can't," they say.

"Well, thank you much," I say, and I left.

So, I tell myself, I'll just find out where he lives and serve him at home. Easier said than done. It was while trying to locate his residence that I found out about all the suits filed against him for many millions of dollars. But I did find his home address. He lives in one of the most prestigious areas of town in a large and gorgeous old home. I arrived at the house and drove around, looking for an entrance. There was a driveway with a vehicle parked in it, and I pulled in. An iron fence with a gate by the driveway had a built-in, heavy bolt lock. I drove around the house, which took up a whole block. There were several more gates. All of them had the same type of lock. In my third trip around, I noted one of the gates was open about an inch. Aha! Another stroke of luck!

I parked right by that gate, walked over to it, checked for dogs, didn't see any, so I opened it all the way and walked right in. Still no dogs. There were two doors on that side of the house, so I picked the closest one and knocked several times. Nothing. I wasn't about to leave, especially since the car in the driveway was an older-model Ford and didn't look like a vehicle our fancy Mr. Jones would drive. It looked like a vehicle possibly belonging to a maid or cook.

I was about to approach the other door when a Hispanic female exited and asked me what I wanted. I told her I was here to see Mr. Jones. "He's not here. How in the world did you get in here?" she said with amazement.

"I came in through that gate over there." I pointed toward it.

"The yard people must have left it open," she said.

I said, "Would you give this to Mr. Jones for me?"

"Oh," she said, "well, yes, of course." I handed her the plain brown envelope with the petition in it, thanked her, and she accompanied me to the gate, saying, "I'll go with you and close this gate."

I left thinking, I'll bet that yard crew gets a piece of Mr. Jones' mind and then some. But I was thanking them from the bottom of my heart!

What are Sons-in-Law For?

I once had to serve a subpoena in an extremely dangerous area of Baton Rouge. I generally don't have a problem with these situations, but this was a really awful area, where druggies and prostitutes hang out day and night. I checked out the area several times, and it was too rough for me. I contacted my client, asking if I could pay a bodyguard type, and they insisted that I do so.

I called my son-in-law, the police officer, who agreed to help me out on one of his days off. We decided that I would meet him at his house, and he would follow me dressed in uniform and driving his police unit.

We got over to the area, which housed two residences in one building, both in extremely poor repair. The yard and porch were strewn with debris, trash, garbage, junk. We both exited our vehicles, me first, and my son-in-law close behind. I knocked on the unit I thought was my guy's. The door opened, and a man told me he was next door. We went to the next door, which wide open. I stepped inside and asked for my subject. A lady pointed out to the next room. My son-in-law remained in close watch in the doorway as I climbed over more debris, trash, furnishings, etc., and handed the subpoena to my man. I thanked everyone, and we hot-footed it out and to our vehicles and left.

My son-in-law told me afterward that he would never have gone to that area if he hadn't had his uniform on, his weapon, and in his police unit.

My Other Body Guard?

I had another similar situation in New Orleans. I first had to locate the individual to whom I had to serve a subpoena. It turned out that she lived off St. Claude Avenue, almost into St. Bernard Parish. To get there, one had to drive along St. Claude Avenue and cross a pontoon bridge no longer in use. Once across the bridge, you had to circle off St. Claude to the right and come back to a small street that ran under the bridge. The residence was there in an area where the homeless and drug dealers and addicts hang out. I checked the area out carefully and decided it would be a good idea to get a young, strong, and muscular fellow to come along.

Back in Baton Rouge, at the law firm for which I was completing this job, they had a law student who was working there as a clerk. I asked the bosses if I could pay Charles to ride over there with me. I picked Sunday morning as the safest time. They said they would not allow me to go without a bodyguard. I presented Charles with the idea of going with me and that I would pay him $100, which was a pretty good deal for an LSU law student in 1997 for a couple of hours work. He jumped at the opportunity.

I wanted to get to New Orleans early before all the residents under the bridge woke up. He was a little put off at my picking him up at 6 a.m., but I told him that was the deal. He was half asleep when I did pick him up, and he slept most of the ride over there. I made sure he was awake and aware of his surroundings as we got to St. Claude Avenue. As I crossed the bridge and made my U-turn to go under, he sat forward in the seat, and his eyes bugged out of his head. I parked in the front yard and was starting to get out of the car when Charles said, "I'll wait in the car." I said, "Like hell, you will! I'm not paying you one hundred bucks to sit in the car! You get out and go with me up those stairs and onto the porch!"

He did and followed right behind me. I knocked on the door and asked for the subject. The lady who came to the door said she was her mother. In these situations, I'm supposed to make sure the subject actually lives there. Sometimes you don't make waves. I gave mom the subpoena and asked her to make sure her daughter got it, and we left.

Charles was back in the car before I was off the porch! My hero!

Serving the Lowlives

I have had to serve several attorneys of lesser character than even the average attorney! Imagine that! A lower than lowlife lawyer. One of these fellows was using mailbox stores, you know, UPS or FedEx types. He was using the mailbox store address and a real phone number. When the number was called, a very charming female voice says, "Mr. Smith's office."

"Is 4444 Bradon, Suite 175, Mr. Smith's mailing address?"

"Yes, it is."

"Is this also his office address?"

"Yes, it is."

In our attempt to locate this lawyer, we found another address that he used a few years back in Plaquemine, Louisiana. In going there, we verified that this was a law firm office for a single attorney, but that attorney was not John Smith. The paralegal here has never heard of Mr. Smith. She called the owner, and we ultimately learned that John Smith, attorney, did use this office as an address but has never entered the building. They had to contact him several times, asking that he discontinue using the address or they would press charges.

I finally just bit the bullet and went to his house. During the week, I had no success, but on the weekend, he came to the door and was so stunned that he accepted service and asked if he needed to sign anything.

But even the sleaziest of types have some redeeming characteristics. While we were on the porch, we noted a Mardi Gras wreath, in April, still on the front door. He said he hadn't yet taken it down because there was a bird's nest inside with four tiny eggs in it. PETA would be proud.

SHOTGUN SALLY

*Sally, Nancy Wilson's ubiquitous sidekick
and partner-in-crime*

The Ard-Angel

It was a cold and rainy day. I mean, the rain was really coming down. A questionable claim had been made pertaining to a stolen vehicle. An engine had been replaced in the car. If the receipt was verified, the claim was legit, and we needed to get a check to this insured ASAP. I had promised my client that I would get the receipt verified today, regardless of the downpour.

As you can imagine, in over forty years of doing investigations, I've driven in all types of weather. This day was one of the worst rainstorms I'd ever driven in. How bad was it? It was so bad I couldn't read the large green interstate signs even when on top of them, but Shotgun Sally and I proceeded forth to New Orleans East. As we approached the city, the weather continued to get worse. If it weren't for GPS, I would not have found the place. In that area of the city, the local highway department does not make it a priority to keep the potholes in good order, I can tell you. In some places, I had to drive on the broken sidewalks to avoid sinking into the ground. But my good old GPS finally announced, "Arriving at the destination!"

The address was 3638 Abundance Avenue. Of course, in this old part of town, there are no municipal addresses on any of the buildings. In this particular block, on the even-numbered side, three buildings were facing me. What I thought was 3638 looked closed. Someone had spray-painted, "Closed. Call 555-6442." I called the number. "We're sorry, the number you have called has been disconnected, please try again." The other building was a residence.

I parked, got out against Sally's wishes, and trotted over to Rick's Glass on the corner. A pleasant gentleman said he'd never heard of FEG Repairs but was kind enough to walk the short block to look for me. Very nice for a New Orleans local. Also, very unusual for a New Orleans local. He came back empty but suggested I speak to Rick.

Rick was much more typical of a New Orleans local, which means he was rude, unfriendly, and did not want to be bothered by this little old lady. Additionally, he was waiting on a customer and was on the phone at the same time. He did ask me what I wanted. I told him I was looking for FEG Auto Repairs.

"What?" he yelled. I repeated.

"What, say again?" he yelled again. So, I gave him "3638 Abundance."

"Slow down," he yelled. "Not so fast, I can't understand you!"

I finally got him to understand me, and he pointed to the building next door. I told him that it said it was closed on the building. He kept shaking his head and pointing next door. He said there was an open door right there, you stupid old woman. Well, he didn't say that, but that's what he meant!

I went back out in the rain, and there was an open door. Well, no, not actually, there was no door. It was a hole in the wall that had been boarded halfway up. I decided to go to Abundance Transmission across the street for some assistance when the overhead door started rolling open! If you've seen the movie *The Green Mile* and you remember that huge black guy, John? The one with the strange powers? Well, the fellow who exited the shop was not that big, but he was close! He ran over to the vehicle in front of mine, retrieved something, and was getting back out to go back into the building when I finally got myself together and got his attention.

"I'm looking for FEG Auto."

162

He pointed to the building with the overhead now rolled open and said, "How may I help you?"

Another nice guy in New Orleans! Wow!

I got my trunk open in the pouring rain and got my briefcase and the receipt as he came over. We did business out of my trunk, which was certainly not the first time for me. I quickly explained the reason for the inquiry, and he said, "Yes, that's our receipt, and yes, we did that work." He was so convincing and confident that I had no doubt. I asked to whom I was speaking, and he said, "Ard," pointing to his name, which was written on the receipt. Wonderful! Even in the pouring rain, I could have gotten down to kiss his huge, wet feet.

So off Sally and I went, back to Baton Rouge in the continuing pouring rain. Most of the vehicles were pulling off to the shoulder by now, and the only ones remaining in travel were the eighteen-wheelers and me! But we got back safe and sound. Well, I did end up with a black eye. I'd like to be able to add that into this story as an adventurous, work-related accident, but, alas, I hit my eye with the latch when I opened the gate to my driveway.

The Pickers, the Stinkers, and the Violent

I've interviewed quite a number of inmates over the years. In almost every case, I look forward to it. In the smaller city jails, you can never know what the conditions are as to the inmates or the atmosphere. It's always a trip. For instance, you have the "Library," as described in another chapter. I have interviewed a few inmates in my local big-city prison without a hitch. In years past, we would meet in the cafeteria, sit at a long table such as seen in the movie *Shawshank Redemption*, with the inmate on one side of the table and me on the other. There was always a guard, who generally sat several tables over.

In recent years, however, things have changed. I would go through the entrance into the facility and explain who I am and who I needed to see. I had to leave my ID with the guard at the gate and could bring only the necessary paperwork into the facility. No purse. No briefcase. A guard would then escort me through several gates and then into the "Interview Room," which was a small room with a desk and two chairs, the inmate on one side and myself on the other. No guard. The door closed.

They'd say to knock on the door if you need assistance. I did wonder about that, but it became the norm after a while. These inmates were mostly Murder Ones who are, according to prison employees and cops, the least violent or likely to escape of all prisoners. And I never had a problem.

In this particular instance, I knew that Inmate Slug was violent. He had been arrested on numerous occasions for simple and aggravated battery and other such fisticuffs-type charges. Most recently, he had hit his mother in the head with a hammer, and she went to the ER with a rather nasty hole in her head. My witnesses shared with me that he used to be a "really nice boy" but had gotten involved with heavy drugs, meth, heroin. You get the picture. Other frequent charges included robberies followed by drugs. His brother told me he no longer has anything to do with him. I guess if my brother put my mother in the hospital, I'd ditch him myself!

So, off I went with my .38 and my protective Sally dog, both of which had to stay in the car. I thought about asking for a guard when I got to my guy, but I'm supposed to be the big and brave lady P.I., so I asked if they could leave the door open—"If you would be more comfortable, of course." I identified "Slug" and immediately took note of the fact that he wore handcuffs. Excellent.

I proceeded to have a productive interview, even though he was all over the map with his version of the theft involved. He complained about the nasty culprits and the creeps who spread untruths about him. I asked him if his mother was out of the hospital and when he last saw her. "The same day that I went to jail," he told me. There's proof of a mother's love and all that!

So, another successful inmate interview.

It turned out that the worst part was the forty-five-minute wait required because all five interview rooms were occupied. I sat in a waiting area with another waiting P.I., who constantly picked his ear, checked it out on his fingers, and picked some more. When he got through with that chore, he proceeded to pick his face and pick at something under his chin.

Watching all this go down was a beautifully dressed female administrative type who must have felt sorry for me. I heard her speaking to someone on the phone in her office, telling somebody on the other line about the people waiting. She came out and told me to go on in. I was most grateful.

The second worst part: The smell! As said, I'd been at that prison many times, but this was the first time I'd been in this section. The odor was similar to a gym locker room, times ten. It was so bad that I carried the smell out to the car, drove home, washed my clothes, bathed, and put on clean clothes. I could still smell it the next day. I guess it was in my nostrils.

I still have an eight-by-ten glossy in my head of that beautifully dressed and coiffed administrator working 9 to 5 in that stink! Does she get used to it? Maybe she goes through decontamination at the end of the day?

I sent her a card. "Thank you for your service."

Horse

Speaking of inmates, I received a letter with the return address of a correctional detention center in north Louisiana. My first reaction was hesitation to open it, not because it was from an inmate, but because of the last letter I got from an inmate, also from Angola.

That letter was sent to me in response to a Letter to the Editor I'd sent to our local newspaper, in which I'd sung the praises of a Baton Rouge blues singer who had a nightclub that was being shut down. The letter said we had the same tastes in music. He was a lonely guy who "would like to get to 'no' [sic] me better" by mail or in person. He signed his name and then shared, "They call me Horse." He ended by promising, if we become friends, he'd tell me why. It was signed, "Kisses."

I did research Horse's criminal record. He was sentenced for pimping, indecent exposure, and indecent phone calls, among others. His letter said he had been in for fourteen years already, and I found he had nine to go. The paper used to insist on name and address when a letter is submitted. They don't anymore, but this means he had my address!

So, it was with trepidation I opened the new letter.

It seems this criminal had been sentenced to federal prison after being arrested in a south Louisiana city in Cajun country. While in the detention center in that community, he was given some type of psychiatric drugs, seen and recorded by a psychiatrist, and ultimately confessed to second-degree murder while under the influence of these drugs. He contacted me because he wanted to have his medical chart reviewed and copied.

His concerns were what kind of drugs he was given, what treatment he received, and how we could get a copy of the recorded statement. He said his mother had hired an attorney, who was supposed to get the judge to allow him to review the medical information but never did. Ultimately, he was sentenced. My first reaction to these types of requests is to ignore them. They are usually from inmates who have nothing better to do. They do a little reading and discussion among themselves and decide they are attorneys. Most importantly, they never pay. He did want to know how much such an investigation would cost.

But I wasn't particularly busy at that time, so I decided to respond. The first thing I did was a background on my client. No surprise, this was not his first rodeo. And it was not his first second-degree murder charge. His rap sheet is some six pages long with thirty-one arrests in this one parish alone. He received a sentence of forty years on this one charge. I told him that I was interested in the assignment. He would, however, need to sign a medical authorization and get $300 to me in advance. As soon as I received these, I would be glad to handle his case. He had related to me that he loved his momma and was a nice guy.

After three months and several correspondences, I surprisingly received the signed authorization and a check from the Baton Rouge Inmate Banking System on a well-established bank. I never expected it. So, off to the detention center I went, taking Shotgun Sally in tow. After all, a case is a case, a client is a client, and 300 bucks is 300 bucks!

Would you Like to Meet my Dog?

When I decided to get a dog, I knew I would get a rescue. There are so many in shelters and, worse, running the streets or mistreated. So, the time came about seven years ago. There is a place in Baton Rouge that gets dogs from the ASPCA that are ready to be euthanized. I went there wanting a small dog, you know, a lap dog. One that would go with me when I had cases in town or in faraway places. One that would sit on my lap as I cruised down I-10.

There was a cute schnauzer puppy with gray hair, the exact color of mine. I don't like schnauzers, never have. They always have that face and chin hair that looks wet or dirty. That said, I have a friend who had a gray schnauzer who was a really sweet girl, and she and I got along just great until she passed. The little girl at the shelter was, they said, about six months old and weighed about eleven pounds. She wouldn't get much bigger, they assured me. I was attracted to her because of my friend's Missy, I guess.

So, my life with Sally began. I took her for a check-over at the vet. Doc said she was probably four-and-a-half months old, not six months, and would get a lot bigger. We had already begun our bonding, of course, so here I am with a 33.4-pound Sally girl who needs a $55 grooming every six weeks and has a constant wet or dirty looking face. But she is the smartest dog I've ever seen. All my past pets have been so stupid. I'm still, seven years later, trying to get used to a dog that's smarter than me! Plus, she is so sweet, great personality, and we are so in love with each other. And all I was expecting was a companion to sleep with me, sit with me while watching TV or reading, travel with me, be with me while I'm on the computer (which she is right now), and sit on my lap as I cruise I-10.

What I wasn't expecting was a Guard Dog and a Protector. Some call her my Sidekick. Others call her Shotgun Sally. What she does do is growl, bark, hit the car windows, and bare her teeth when she thinks we are possibly being threatened. She has never bitten anyone, nor do I think she ever would, unless I was attacked, and she could get to the attacker. But when someone she doesn't know comes to our house or car, she sure puts on a good show. So, since I've had Sally, I've never had a problem with a stranger.

Several years ago, I had a case in the Ninth Ward in New Orleans. Since Katrina, everyone knows the Ninth

Ward. I had to interview a witness. When I got to his residence, we noticed two guys sitting on a curb about half a block down the street. I chose to do my interview outside, standing between my car and his front door. Sally stayed alert in the driver's seat, staring down the two guys who stared back at her. They did not move. I felt relaxed, comfortable, and safe.

A time before that, I was to meet with my customer in a really bad area of Baton Rouge to interview a policyholder who was claiming the theft of four AC units from his four-plex rental. The night before the scheduled meeting, there was a murder one block over. My customer called me that morning and admitted that he was too scared to go there. So, off Sally and I went by ourselves.

My usual approach in this circumstance is to get there early enough to question neighbors to learn if they saw or heard anything concerning the alleged theft. I exited my car, leaving Sally in her usual spot on the driver's seat. I saw a male about a block away walking toward us. Sally started her big show, and he turned around, going back from whence he came. Again, I felt relaxed and comfortable, knocking on doors and walking around the four-plex, taking pictures of where the AC units had been. As an aside, my customer ended up having to pay the claim. Would you believe, some months later, the same claimant submitted the same claim again? Four AC units allegedly were stolen from the same apartment complex. As it turned out, he never replaced the units the first time.

Very recently, I was at McDonald's, getting a bite to eat. I placed my to-go order inside. There was a fellow who had placed his order before me having trouble getting his money out of his pocket. I made casual speak about having similar difficulties, after which I noted his appearance and realized he was a vagrant. After I got settled in my vehicle and started eating, there was a knock on my window.

Sally had started barking, growling, baring her teeth, and hitting the windows, as I cracked the one at the driver's side. There was the vagrant, who said, "Do you know what's beautiful?" I told him to have a nice day as Sally growled at him to hit the road. I guess he was trying to decide if he could con this little old lady or something but didn't ponder too long since Sally continued putting on her show. He took off, walking toward the parking lot down the street, where a lot of men hang out, waiting to be asked if they wanted to work. I'm still wondering, "What's beautiful?" Probably a twenty-dollar bill.

But here's my all-time favorite Sally story. After you turn sixty-five, some people think you automatically become simpleminded, stupid, and have no common sense. This particular day I was leaving Wal-Mart and putting my stuff in my car trunk when a preppy-type female, probably in her forties, pulled up in her SUV right behind my parked vehicle. She opened her window and excused herself, saying she had noticed I had left my dog in my car. She wanted to explain to the little old gray-haired simpleton that I shouldn't leave my dog in my vehicle.

"You know, there are people who steal cars. They go up to a car and knock out a window and steal your belongings or your car. They break the window, get in your car, and can drive off with your dog. You just shouldn't leave your dog in your car like that!" and she went on and on and, finally, "So I think you'd be better off just leaving your little dog at home!" She continued along these lines, going on and on.

When she finally took a breath, I said, very sweetly, "Thank you so much for your concern. Could I ask you something? Would you like to get out and meet my little girl?"

"Sure!" she said. She got out and started approaching my vehicle. Sally introduced herself in grand style, barking, growling, baring of teeth, nose on the windows closest to where she was. The lady jumped back, hand over mouth, and said, "Oh my God!"

I smiled and informed her, "I take my 'little dog' everywhere I go, especially to high crime and drug-traffic areas. She keeps me safe while I work. By the way, I am a private investigator. I investigate insurance claims. You know, like when someone smashes your car window, breaks into your car, and steals your stuff, or when someone steals your vehicle? I take my dog with me as my protection. And she is very protective, as you can see. So, the next time you decide to be a busybody and interfere with someone else's life, perhaps you will think twice before you say something stupid."

CASE CLOSED

PostScript

After Nancy passed away in 2019, Shotgun Sally retired and is no longer doing investigations. She has embarked on a new adventure in the Texas Hill Country chasing deer, hunting squirrels, and unlearning how to be a guard dog.

Made in USA - Kendallville, IN
1171608_9781735670201
09.29.2020 0914